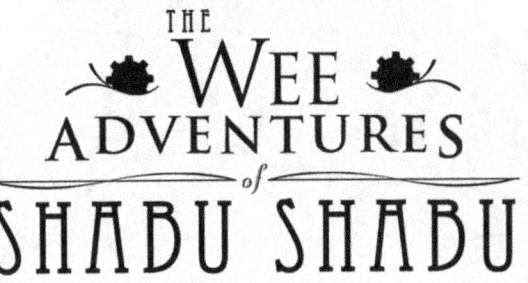

I0477462

COLORING BOOK
VOLUME 1

Illustrated by Michael Csokas

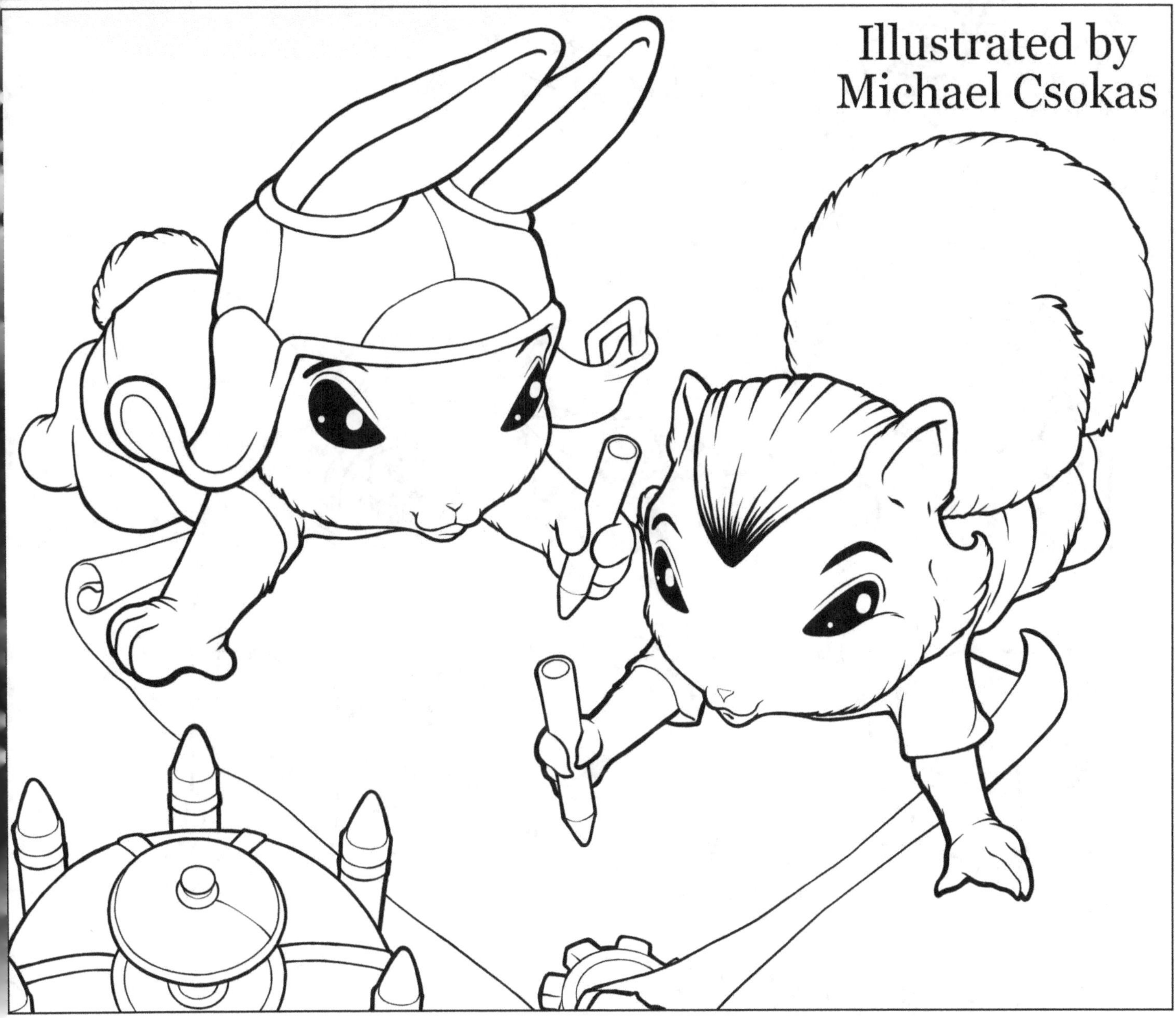

THE WEE ADVENTURES OF SHABU SHABU™ – COLORING BOOK – VOLUME 1

Copyright © 2014 by Steam Powered Productions Pte Ltd
ISBN: 978-981-09-2417-1

For permission requests, write to the publisher, addressed
"Attention: Permissions Coordinator,"
at the address below.

Steam Powered Productions Pte Ltd
info@shabusworld.com
www.shabusworld.com
www.facebook.com/TheWeeAdventuresofShabuShabu

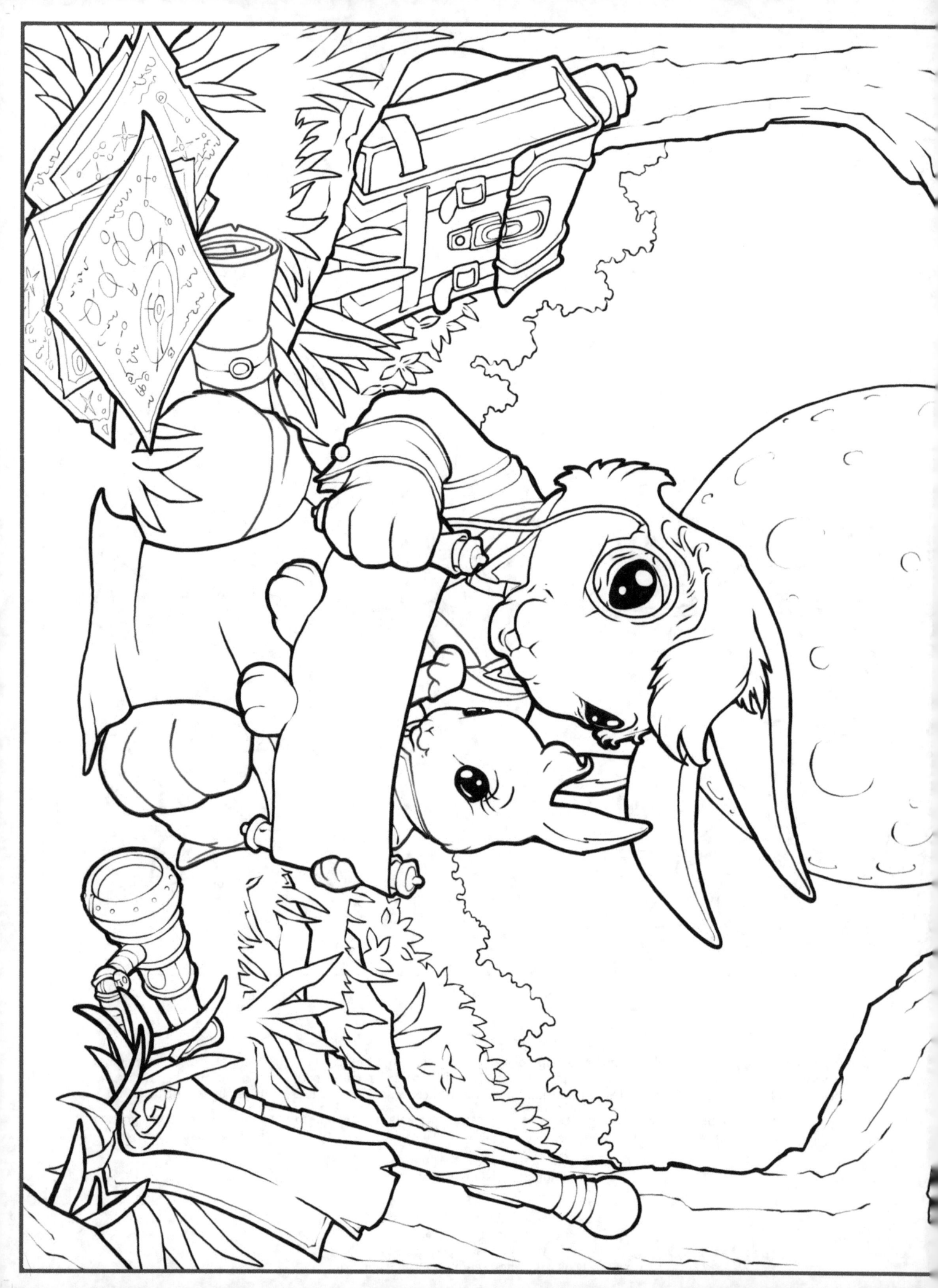

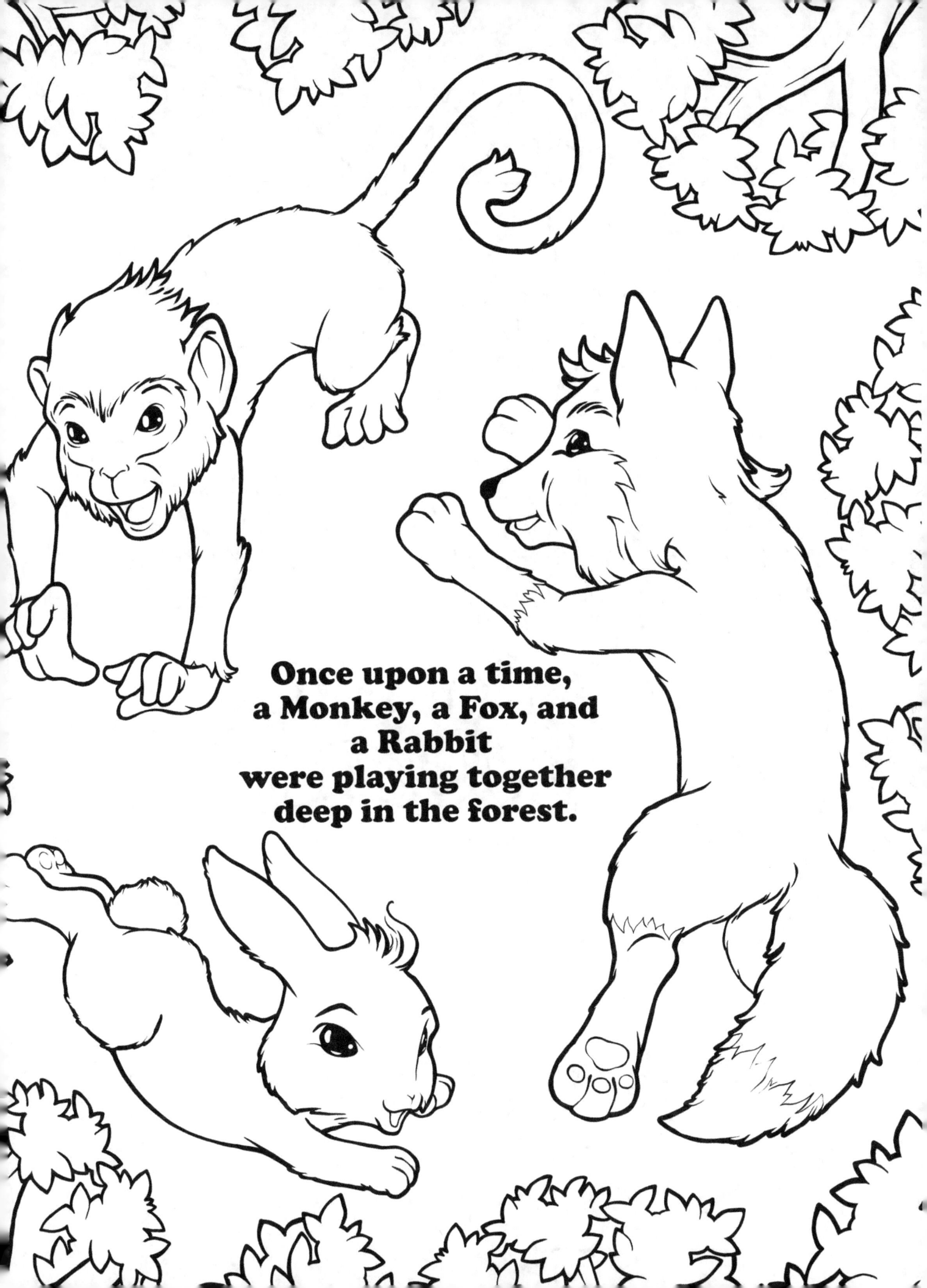

Once upon a time,
a Monkey, a Fox, and
a Rabbit
were playing together
deep in the forest.

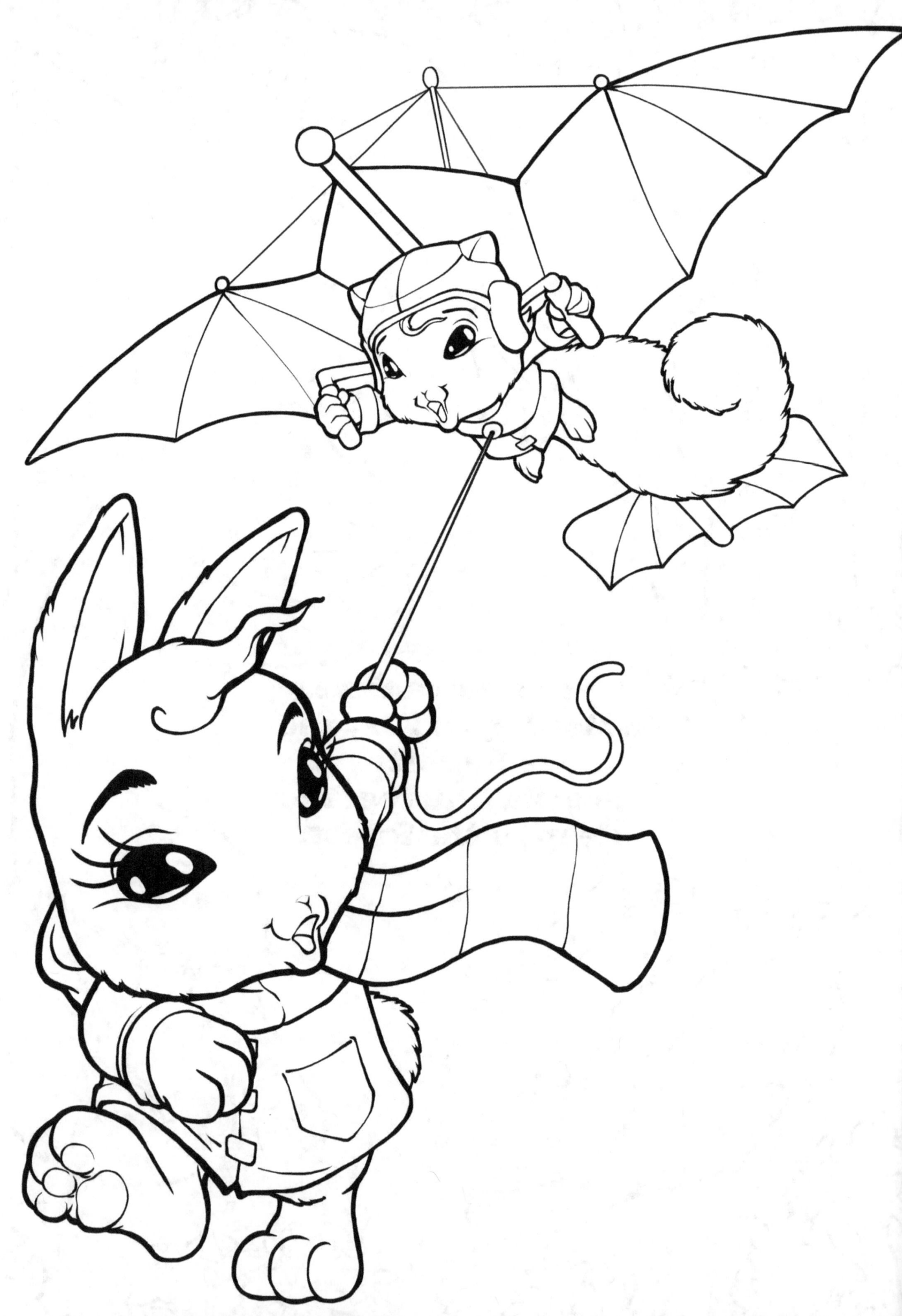

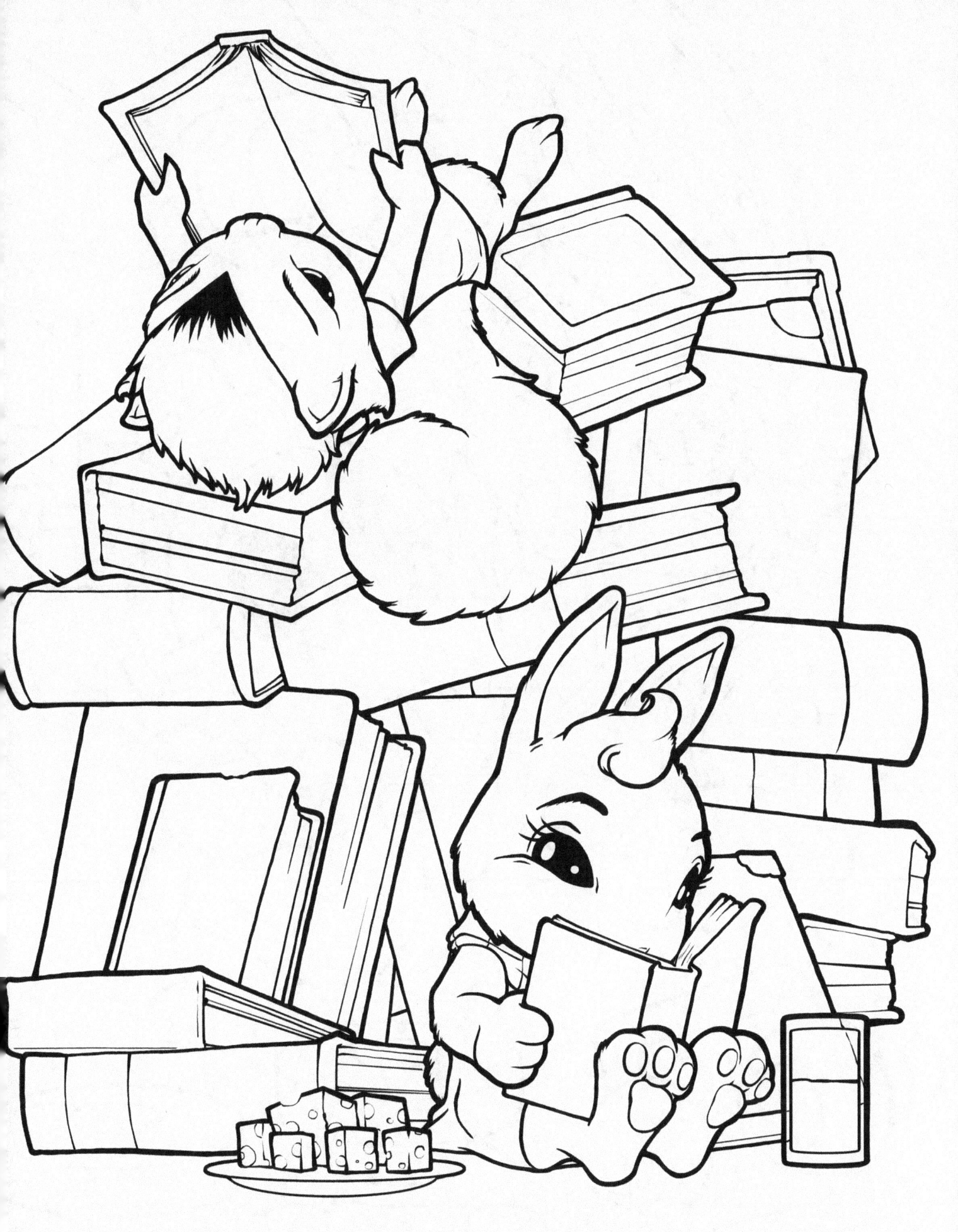

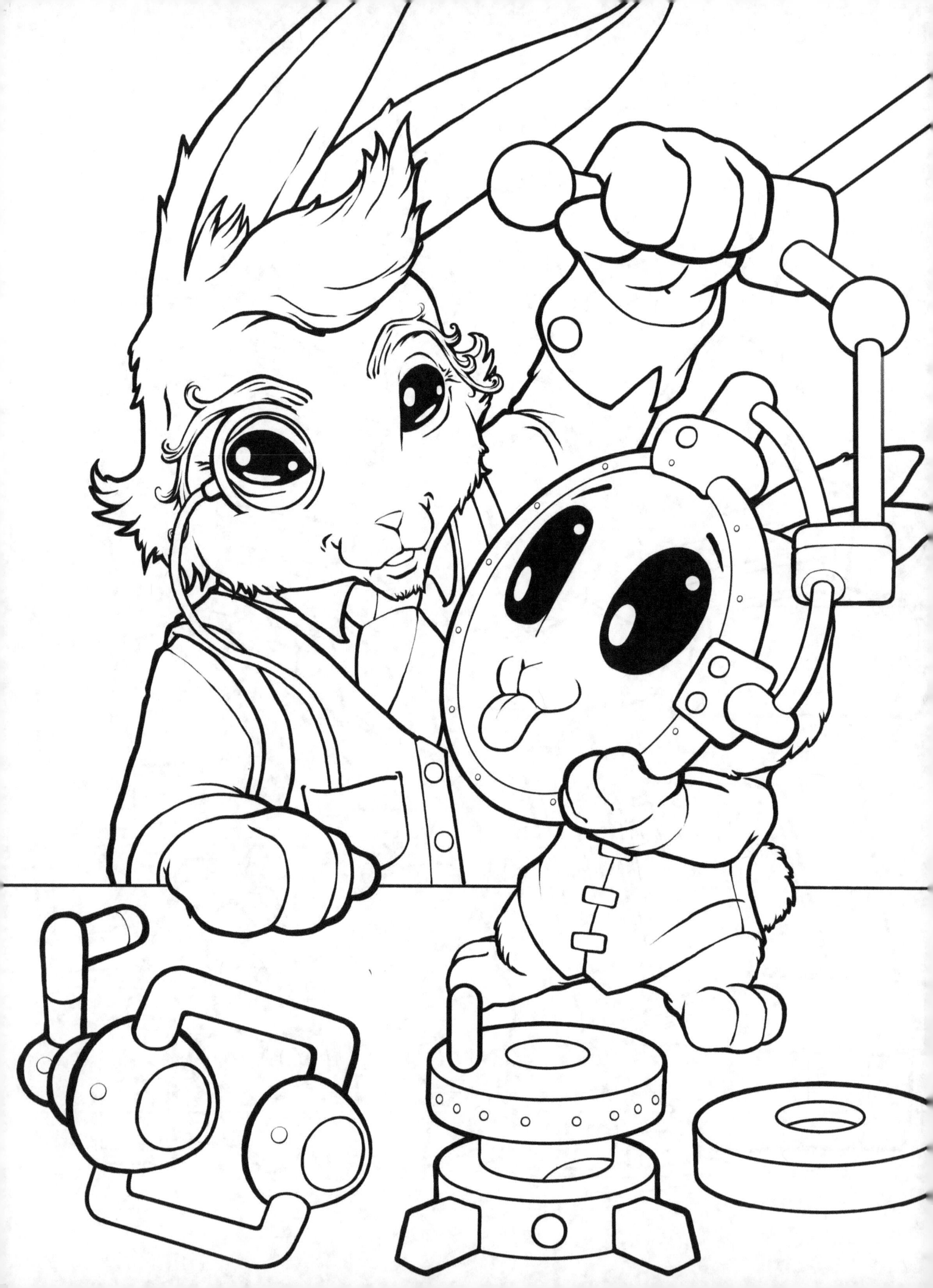

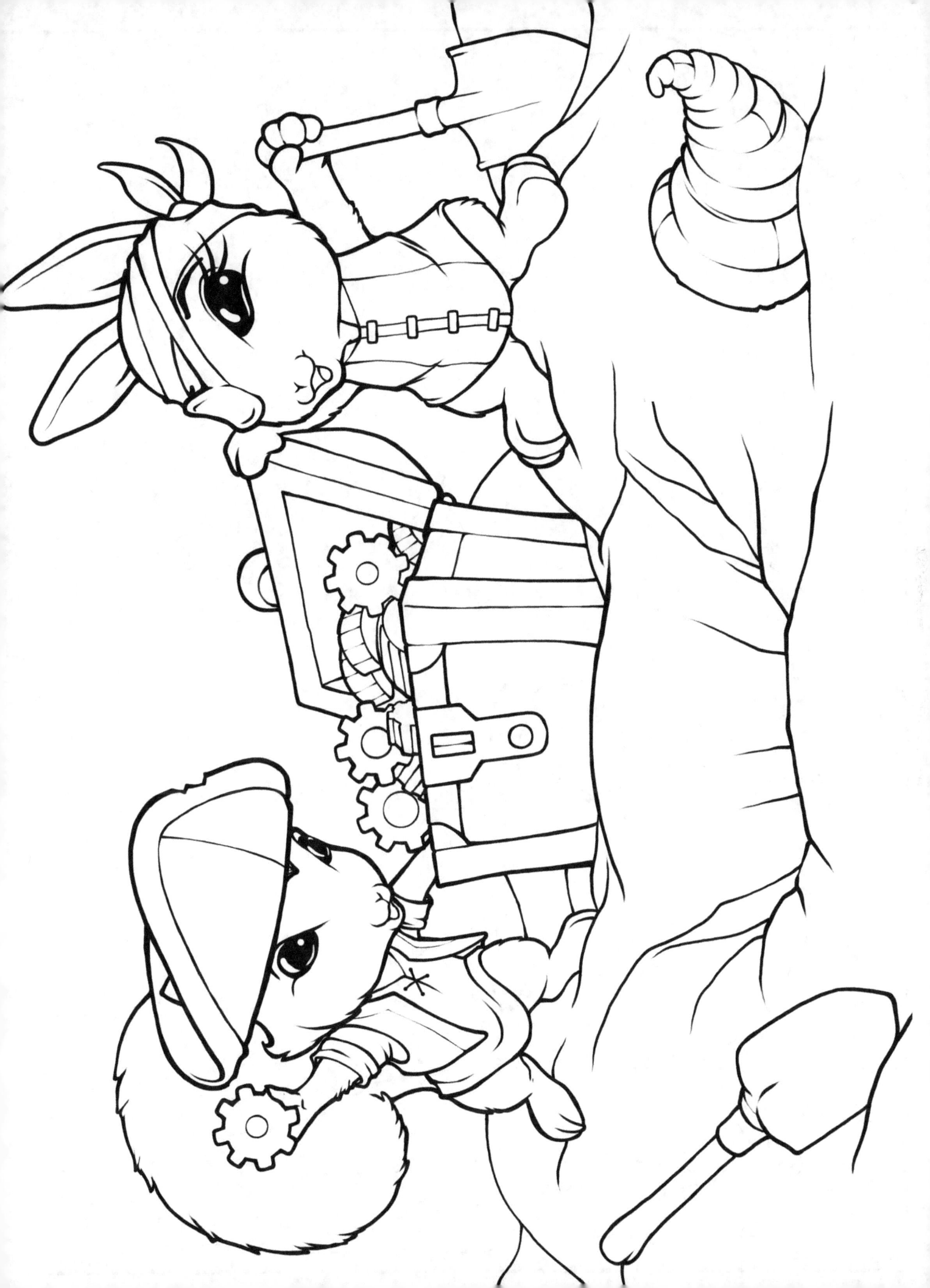

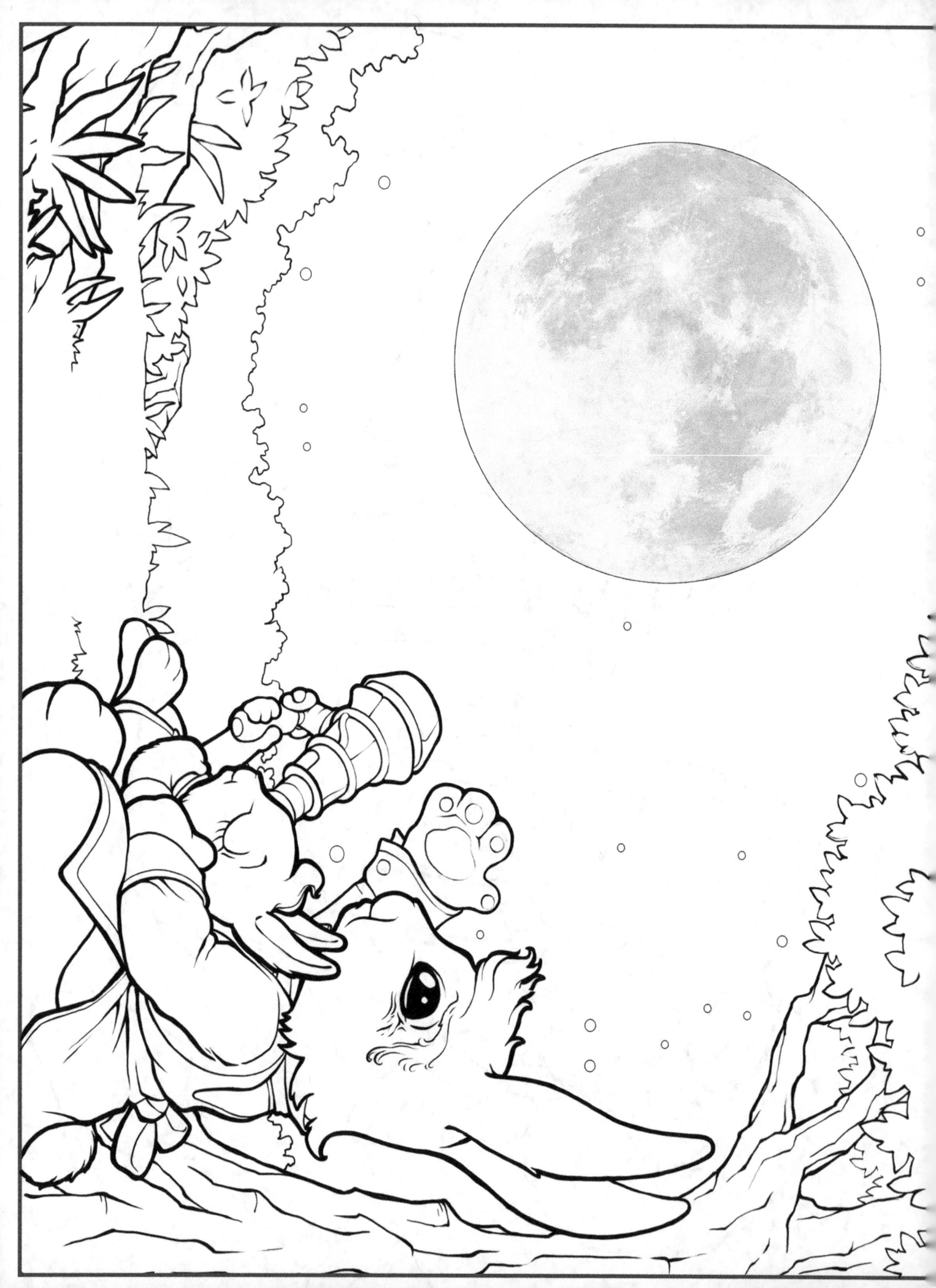

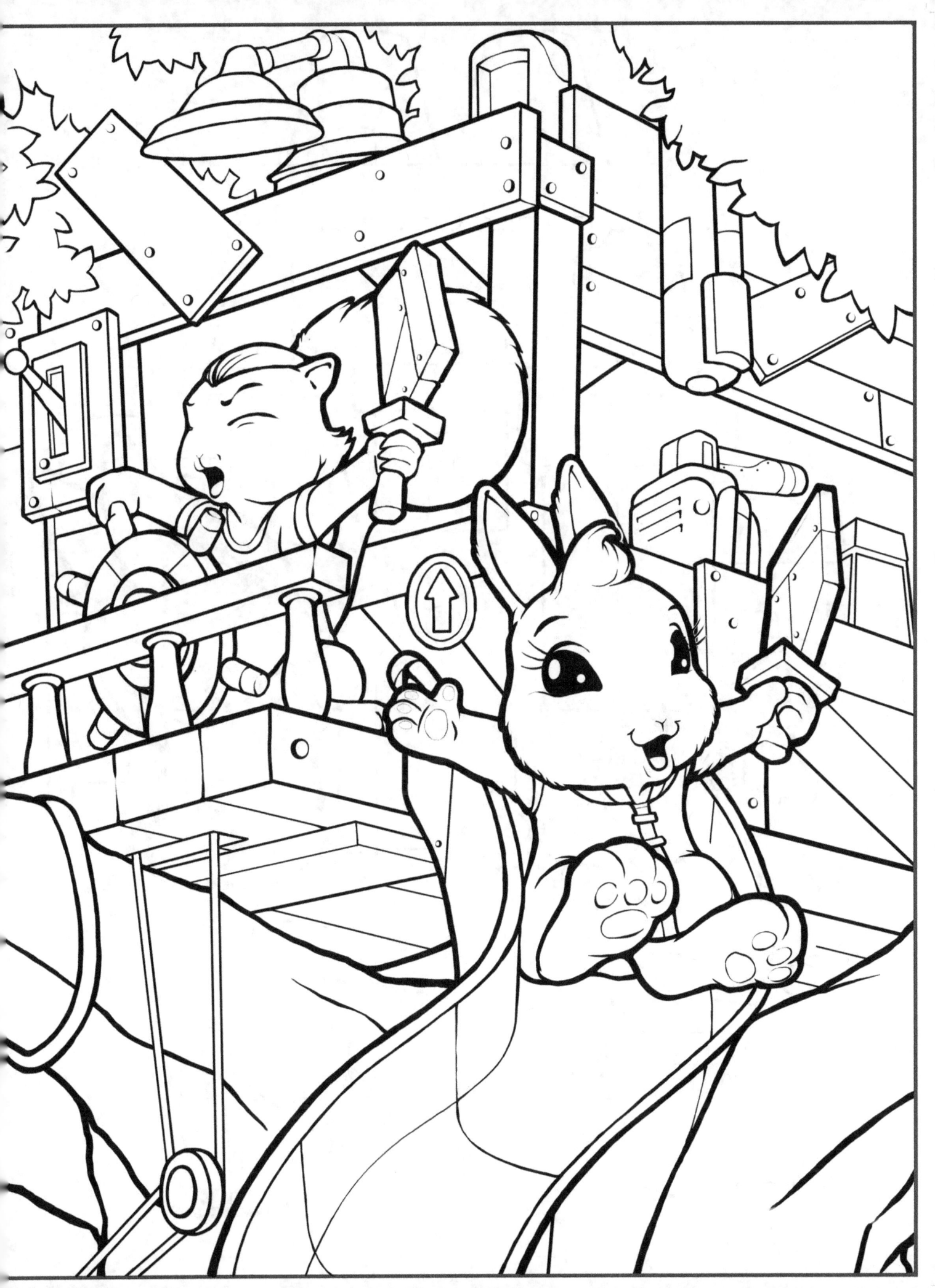

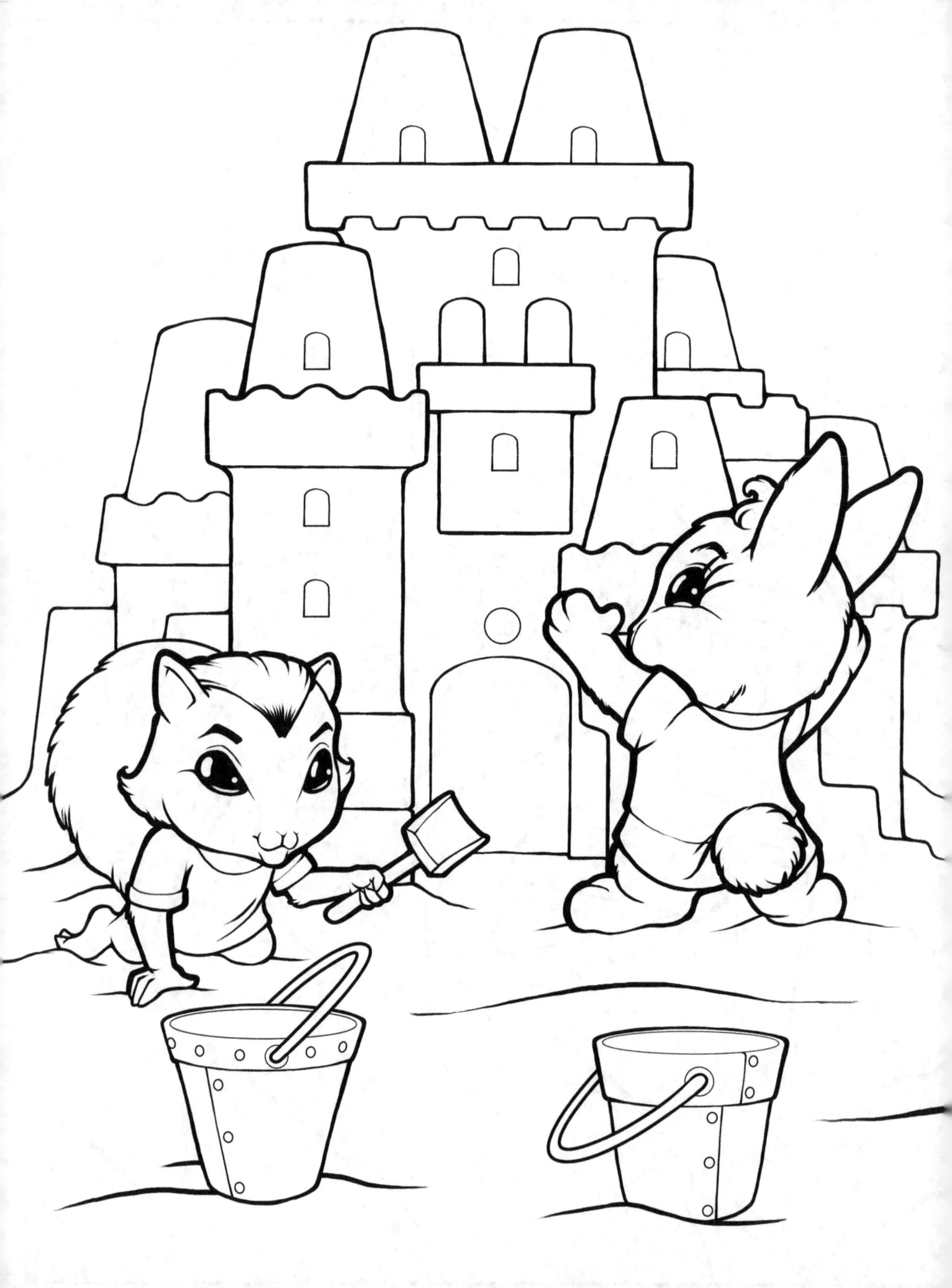

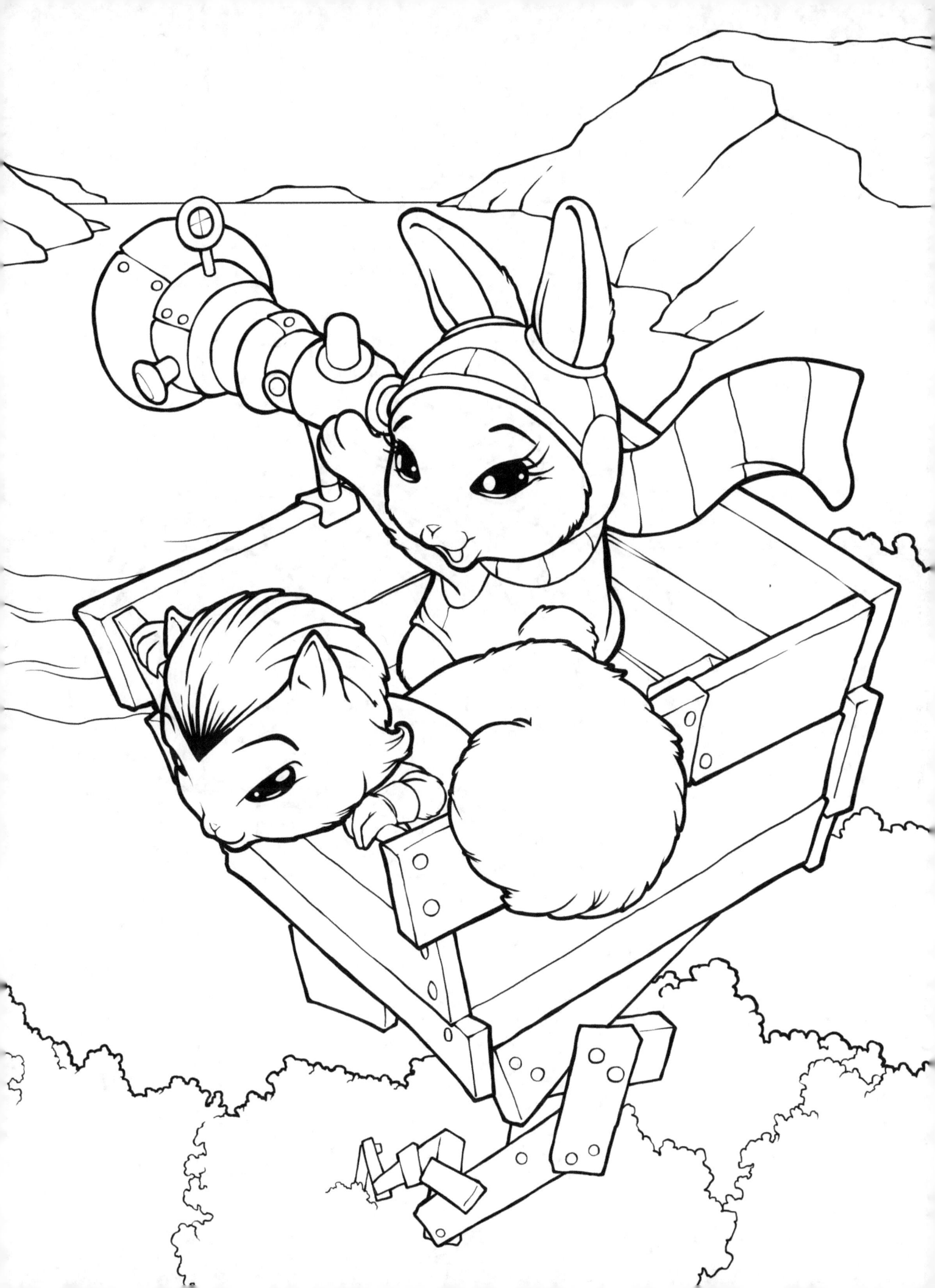

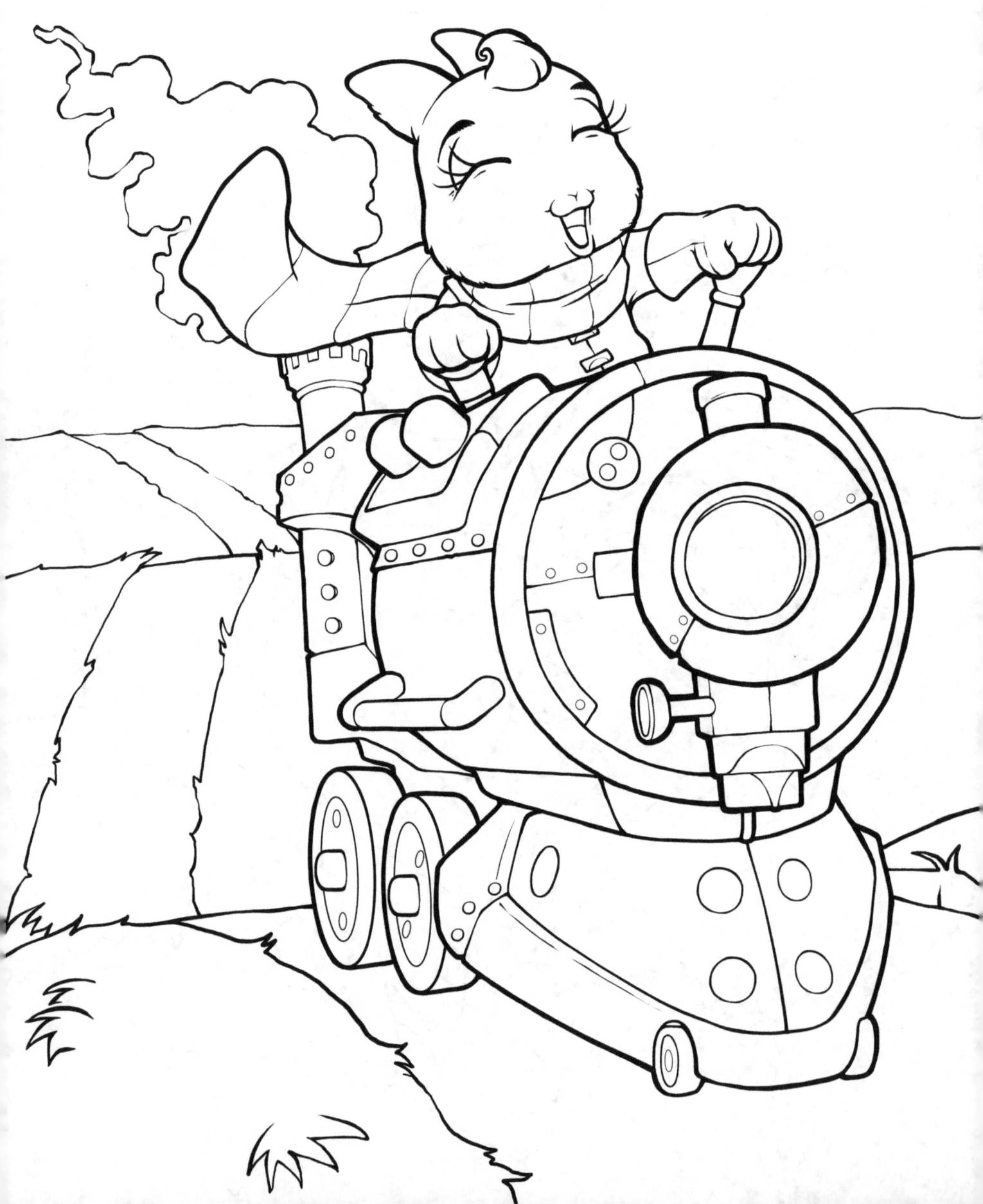

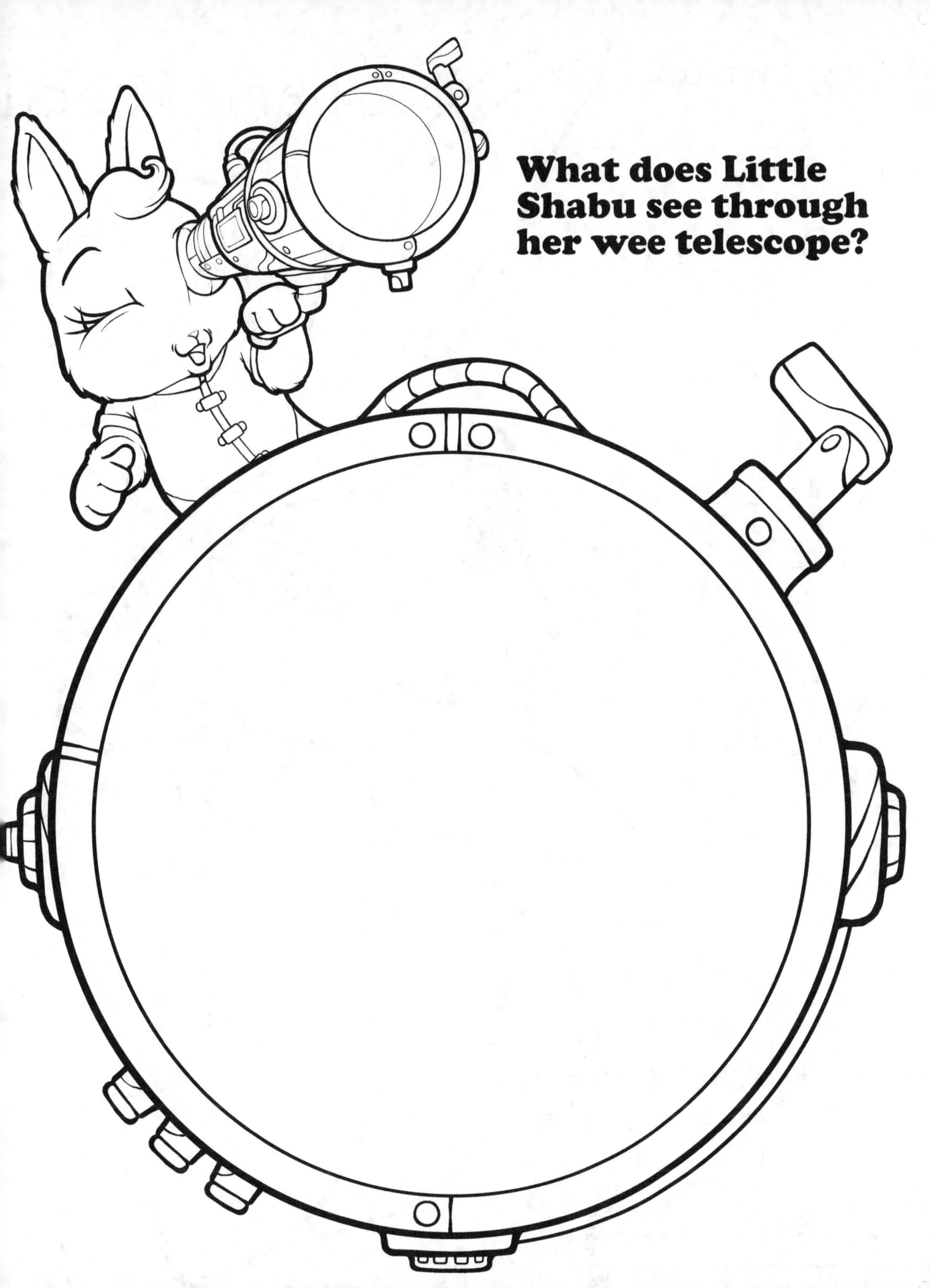

What does Little Shabu see through her wee telescope?

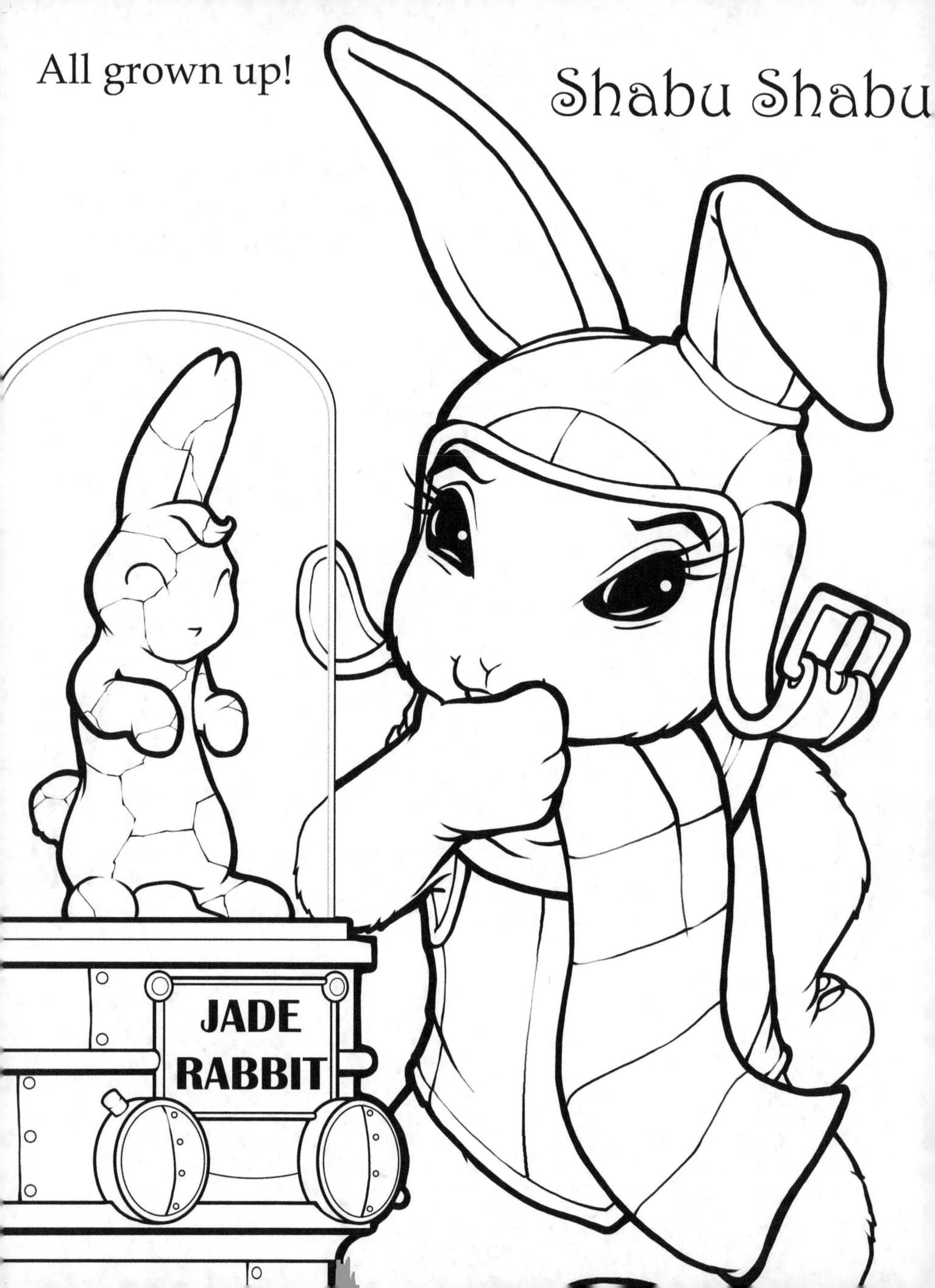

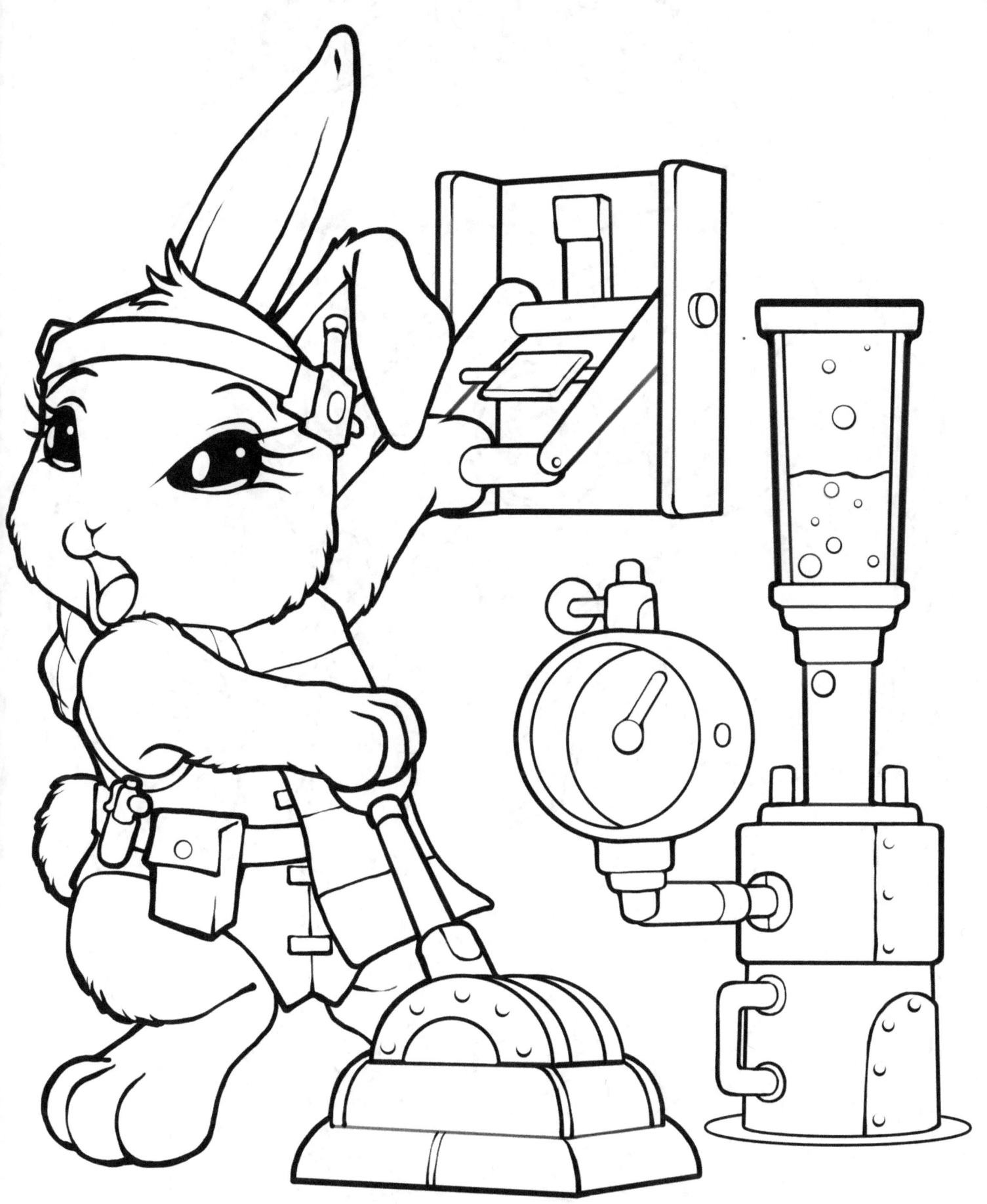

All grown up!

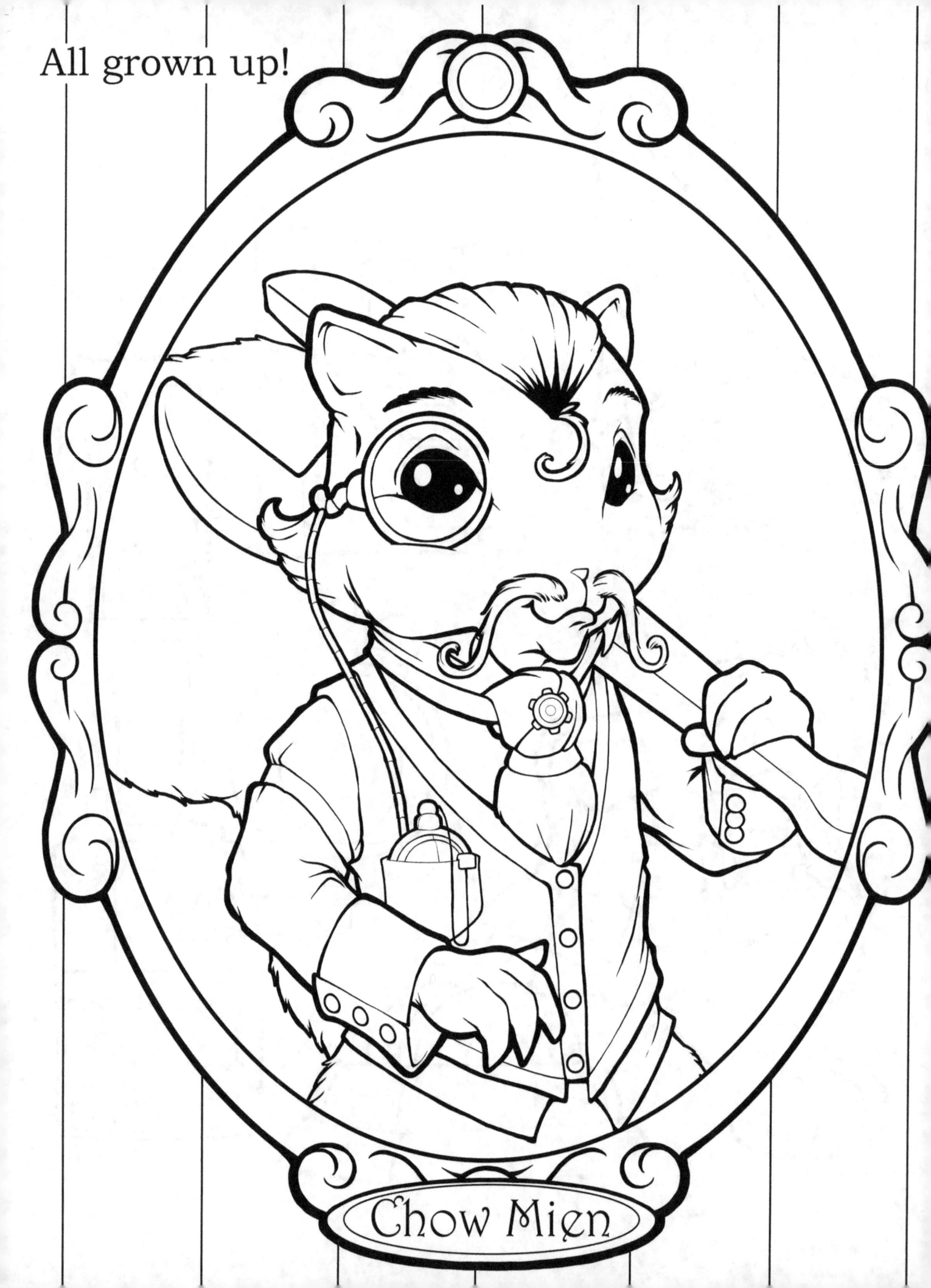

Chow Mien

Messenger Mouse

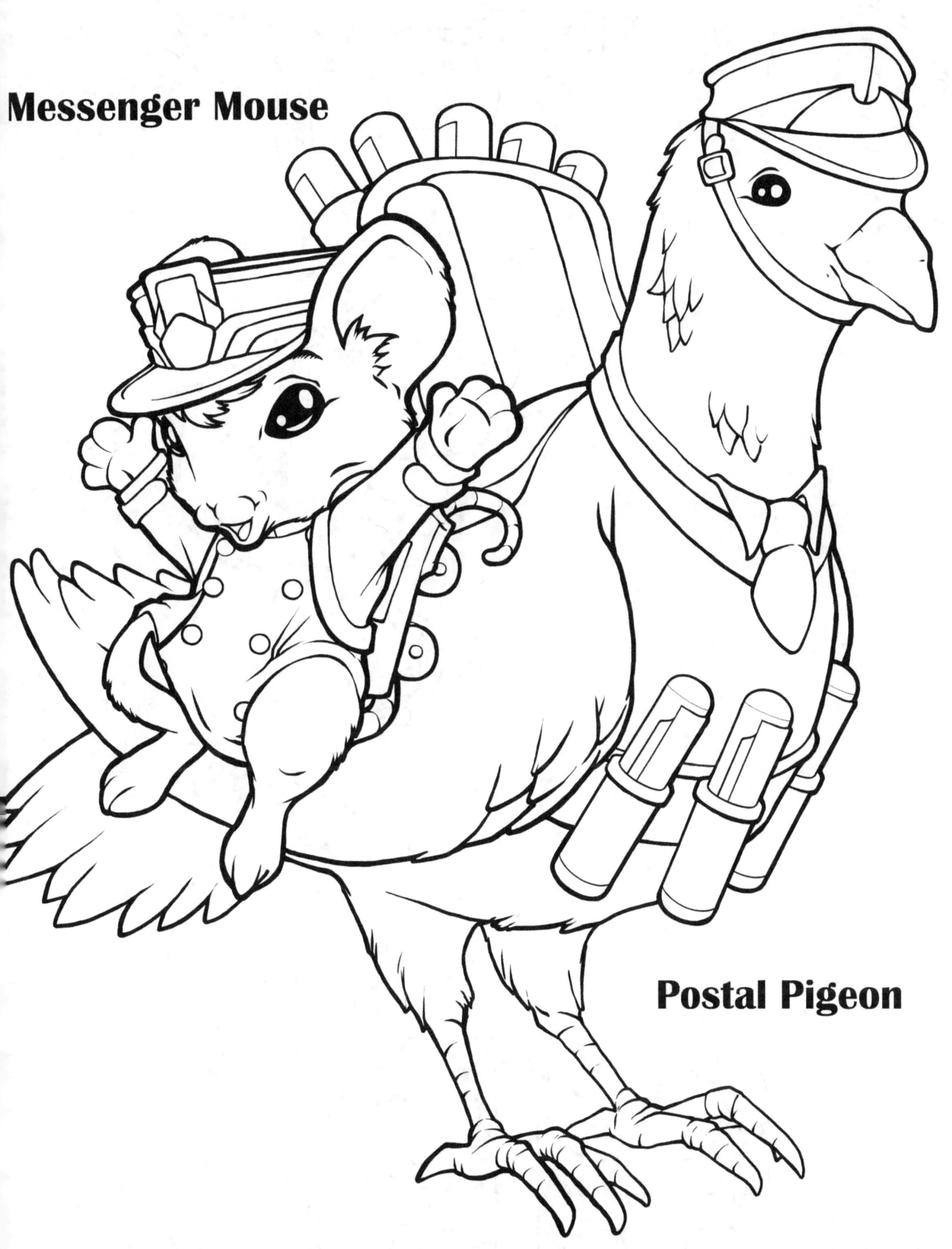

Postal Pigeon

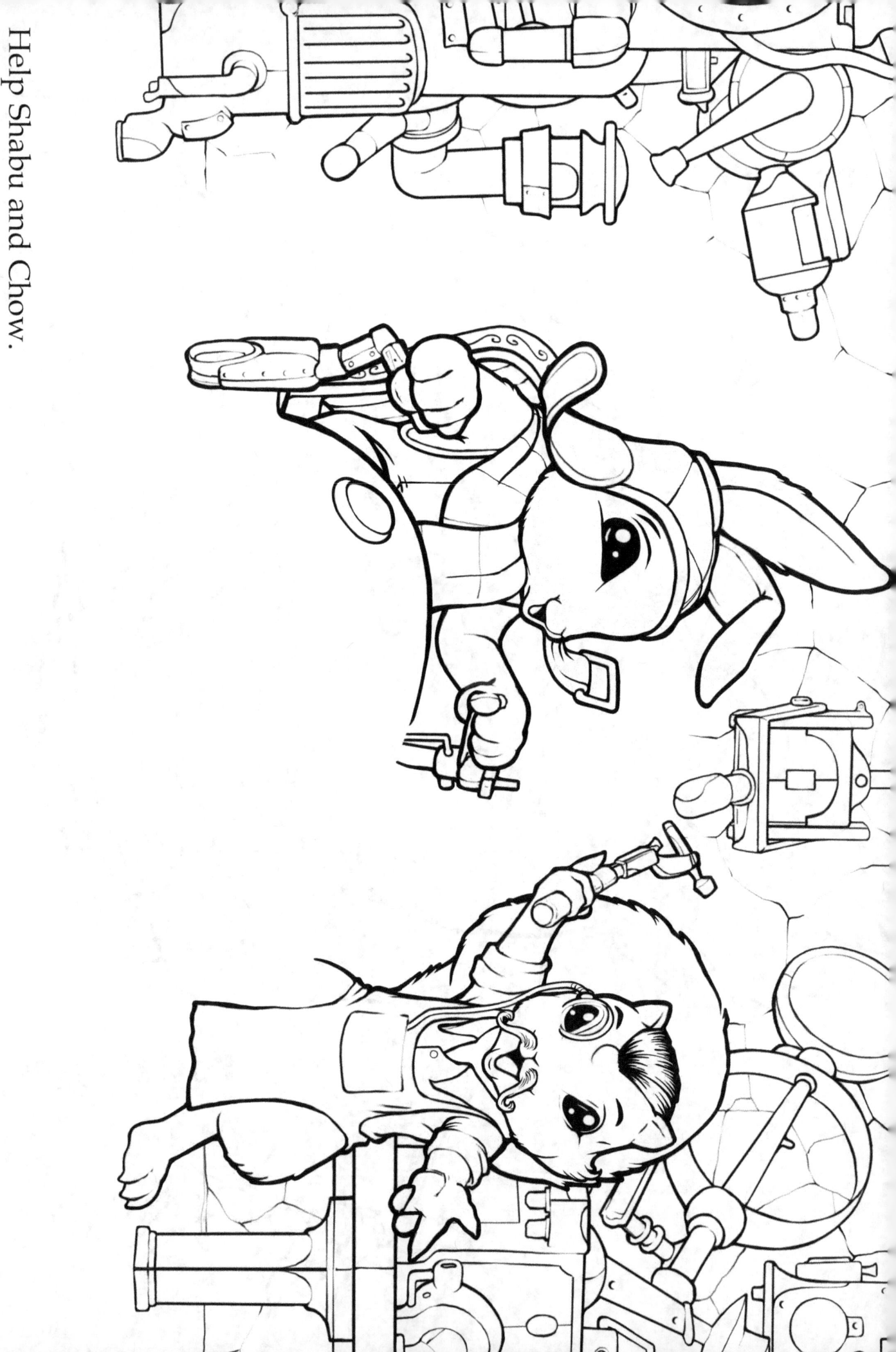

Help Shabu and Chow.
Draw a picture of what
the friends have invented.

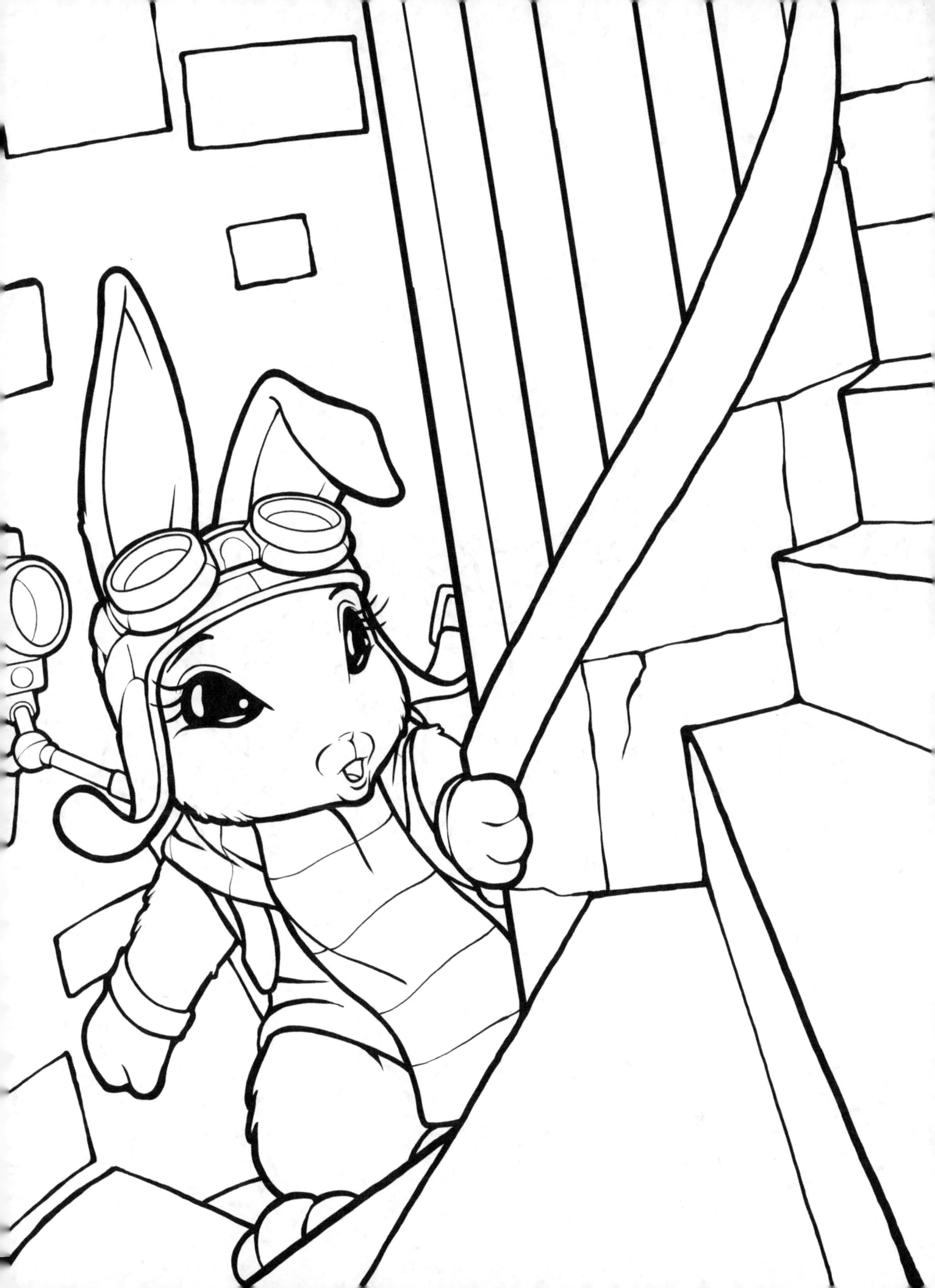

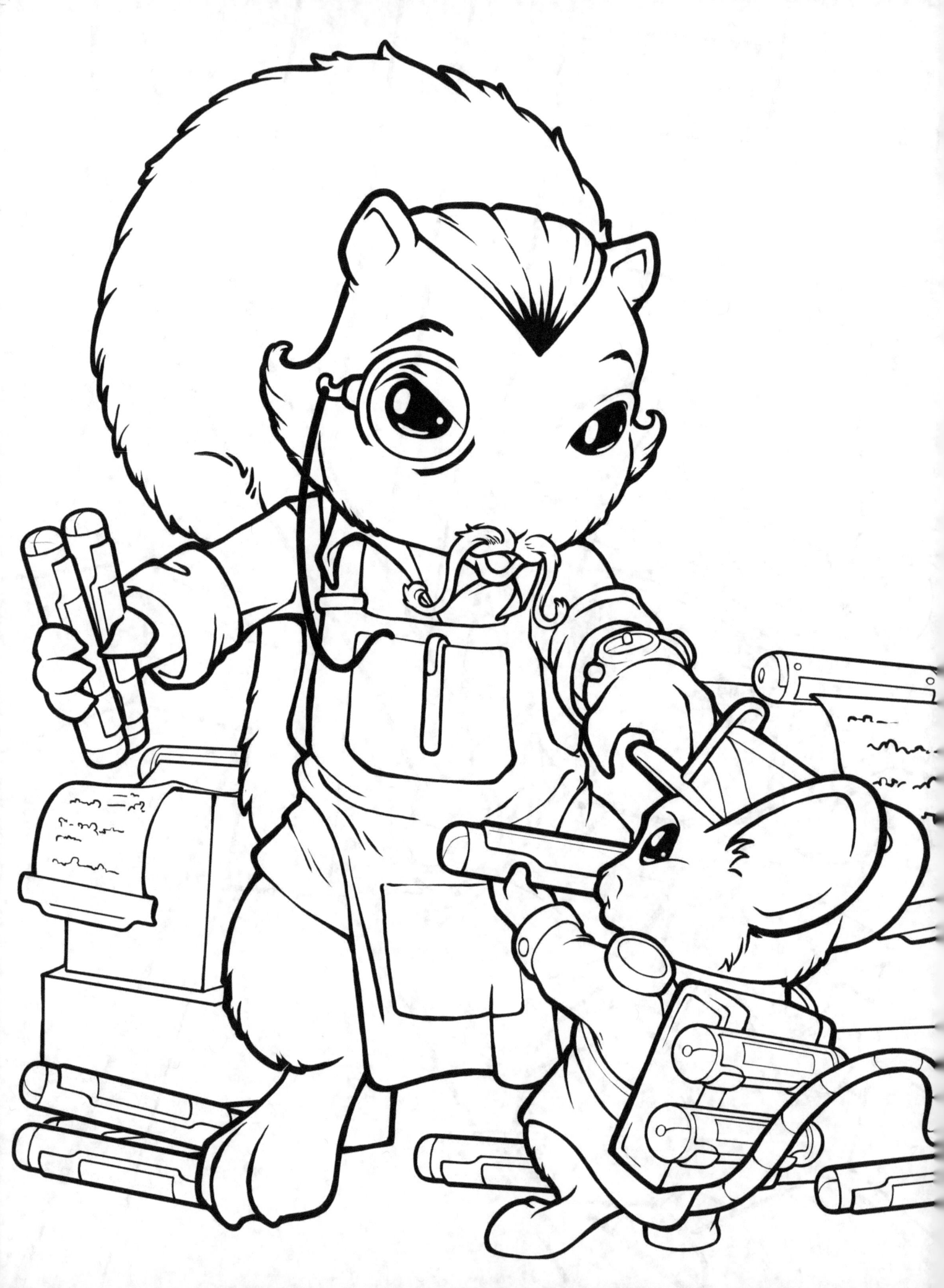

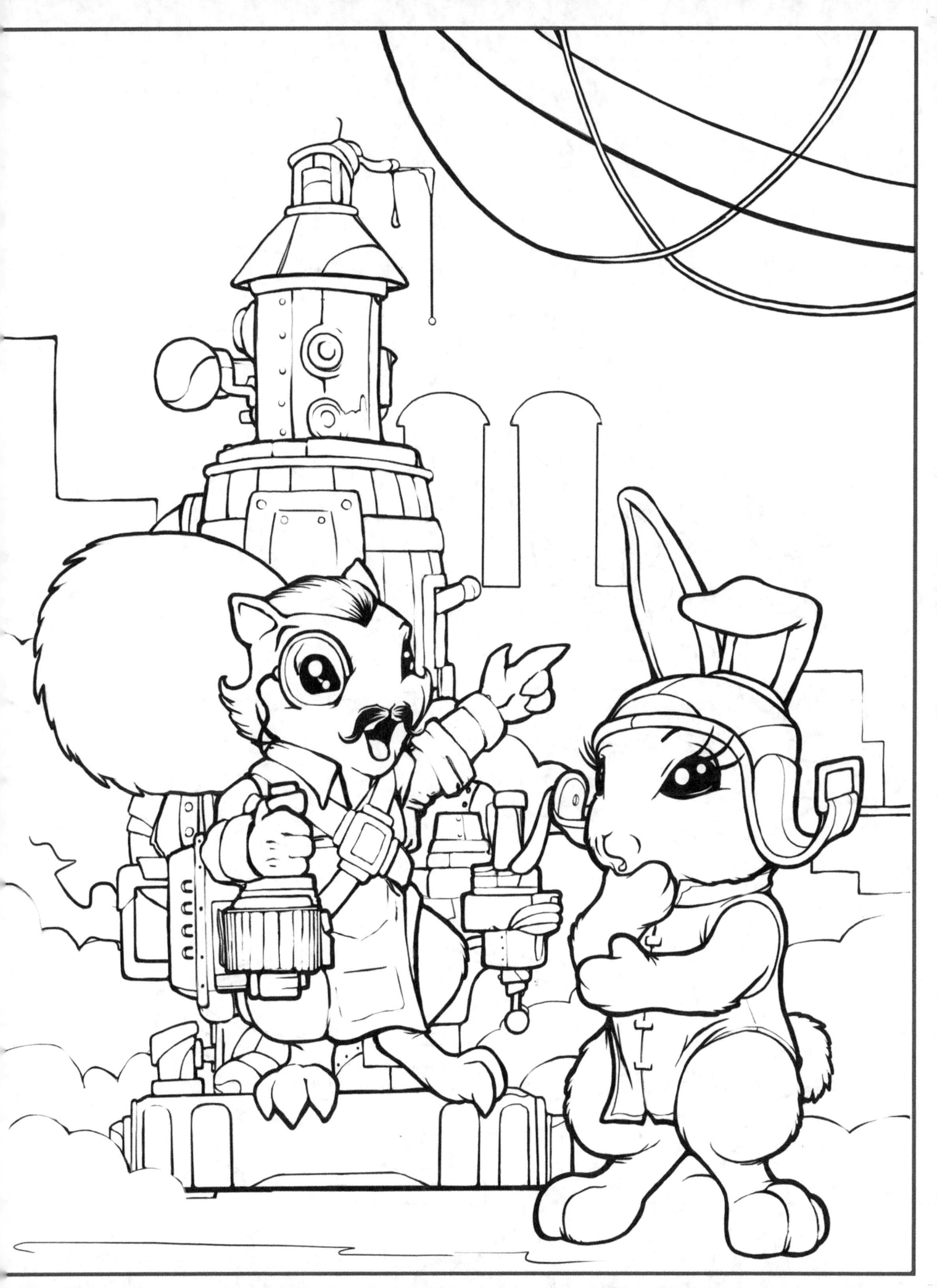

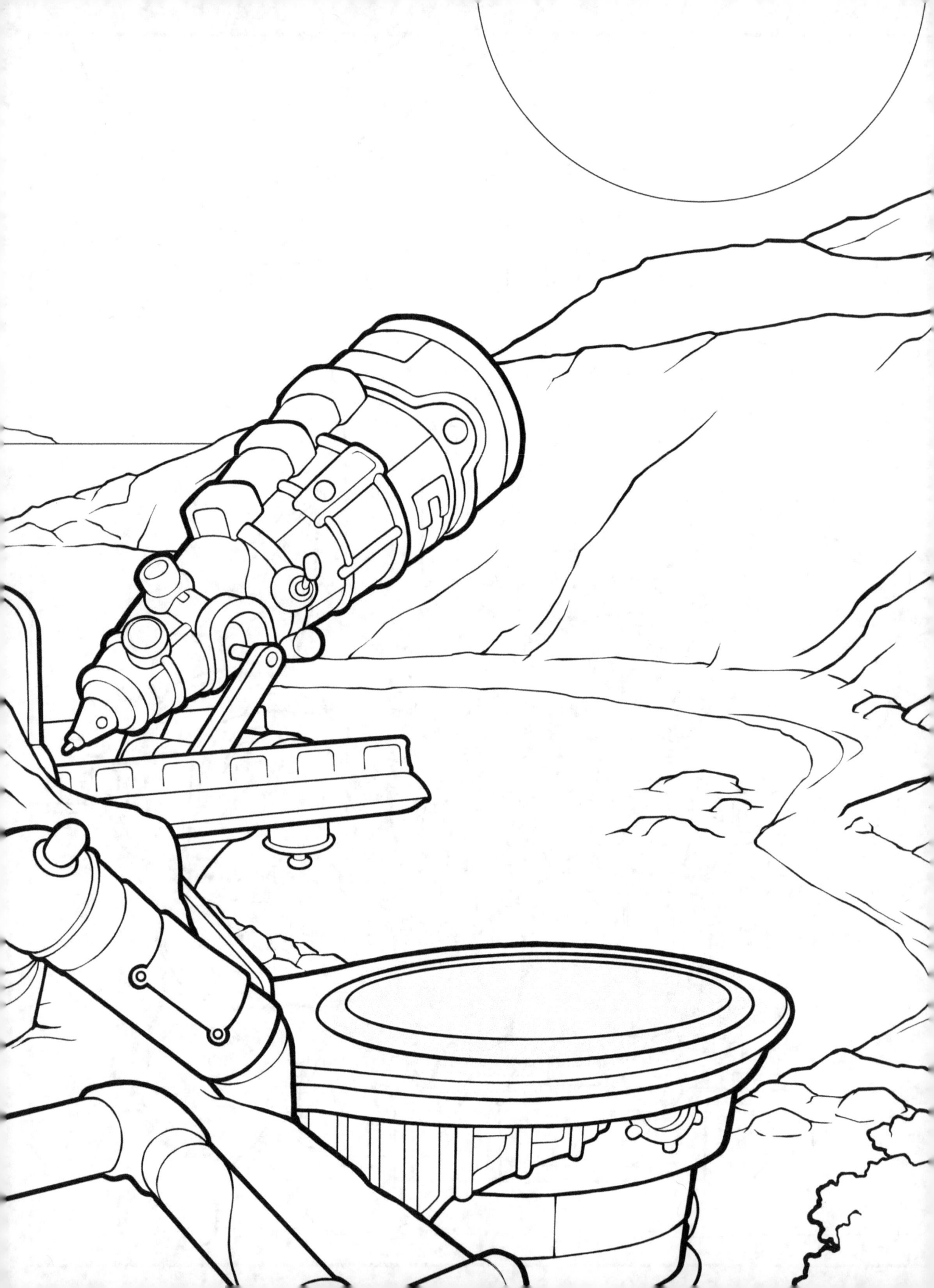

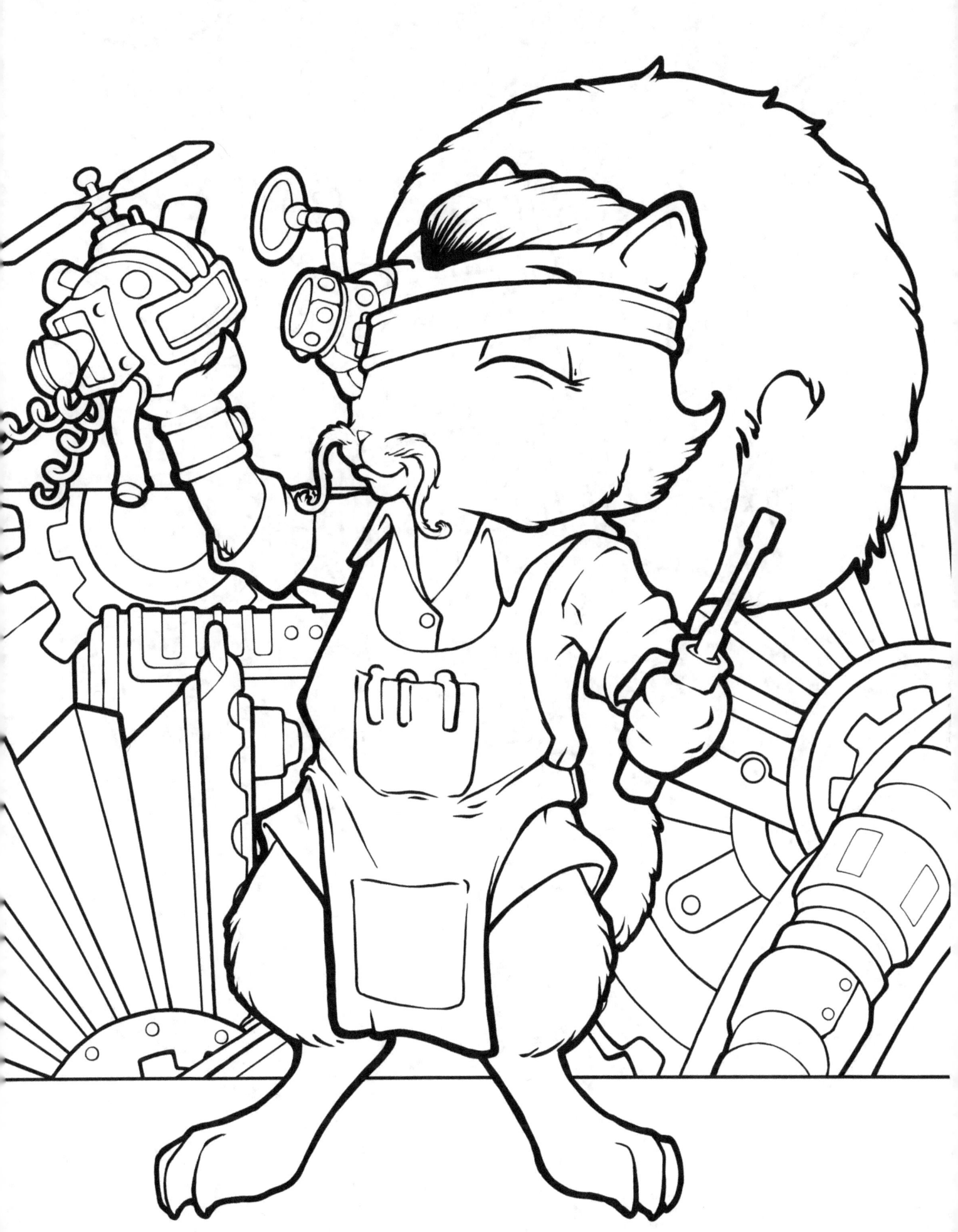

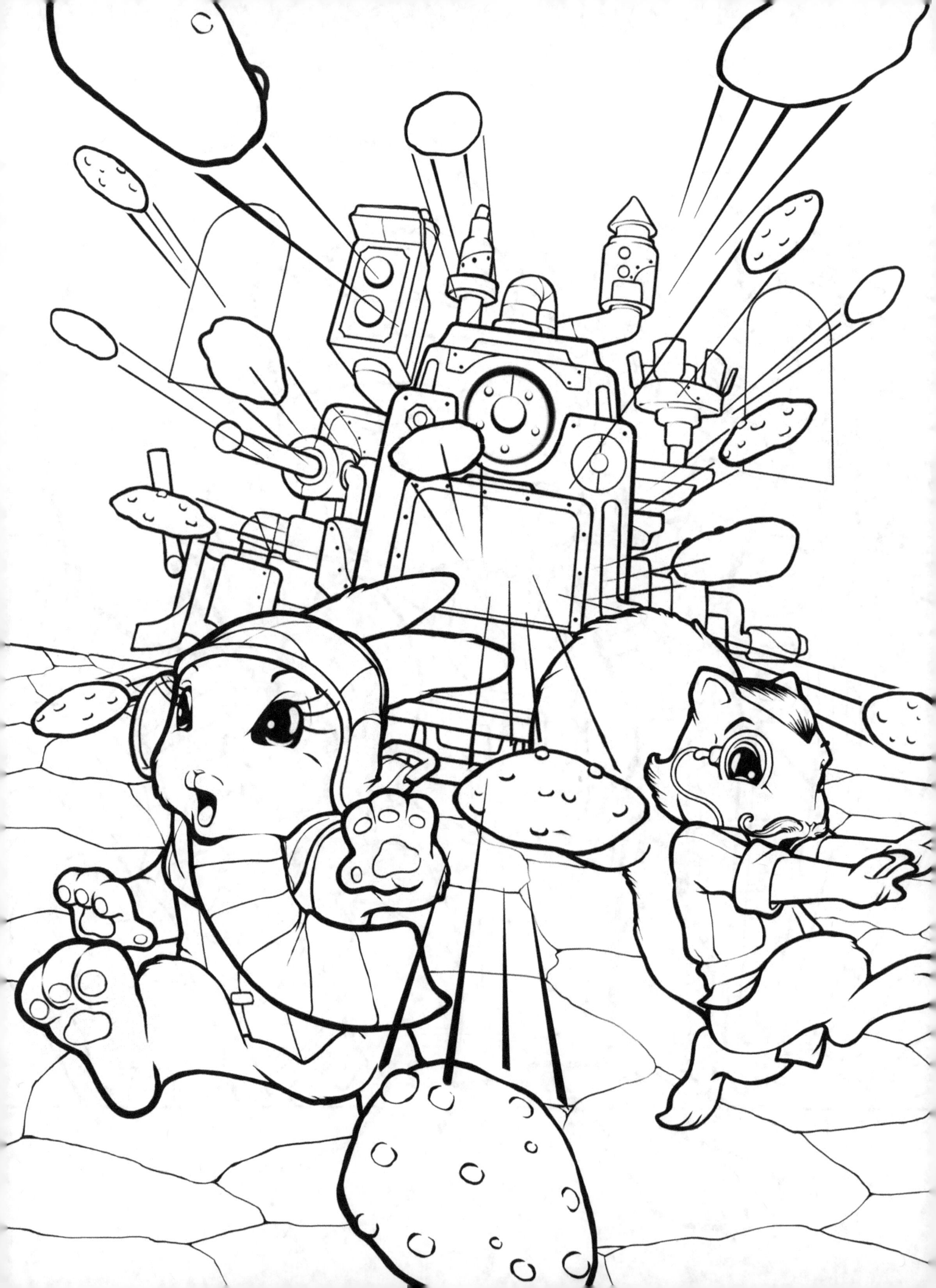

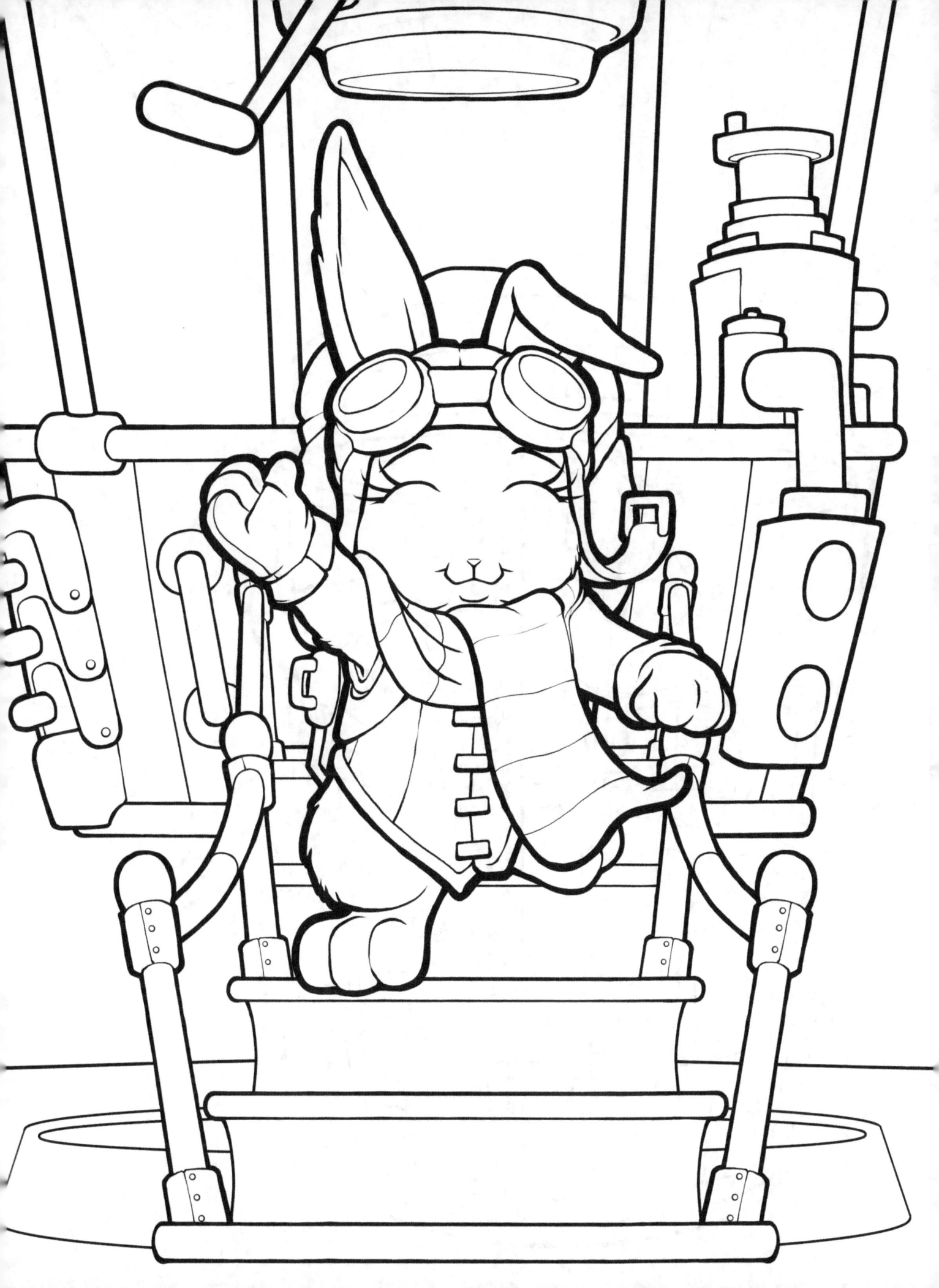

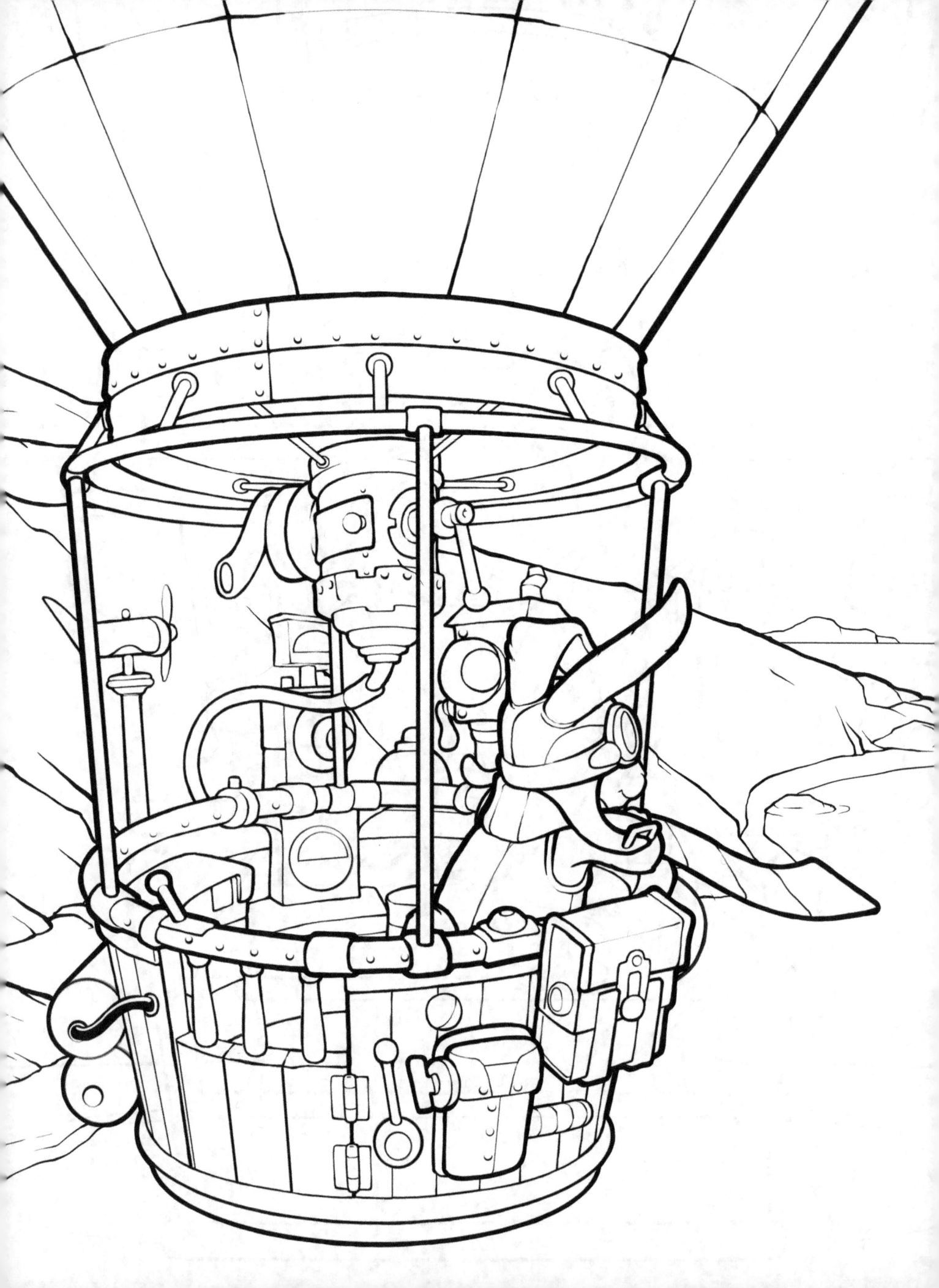

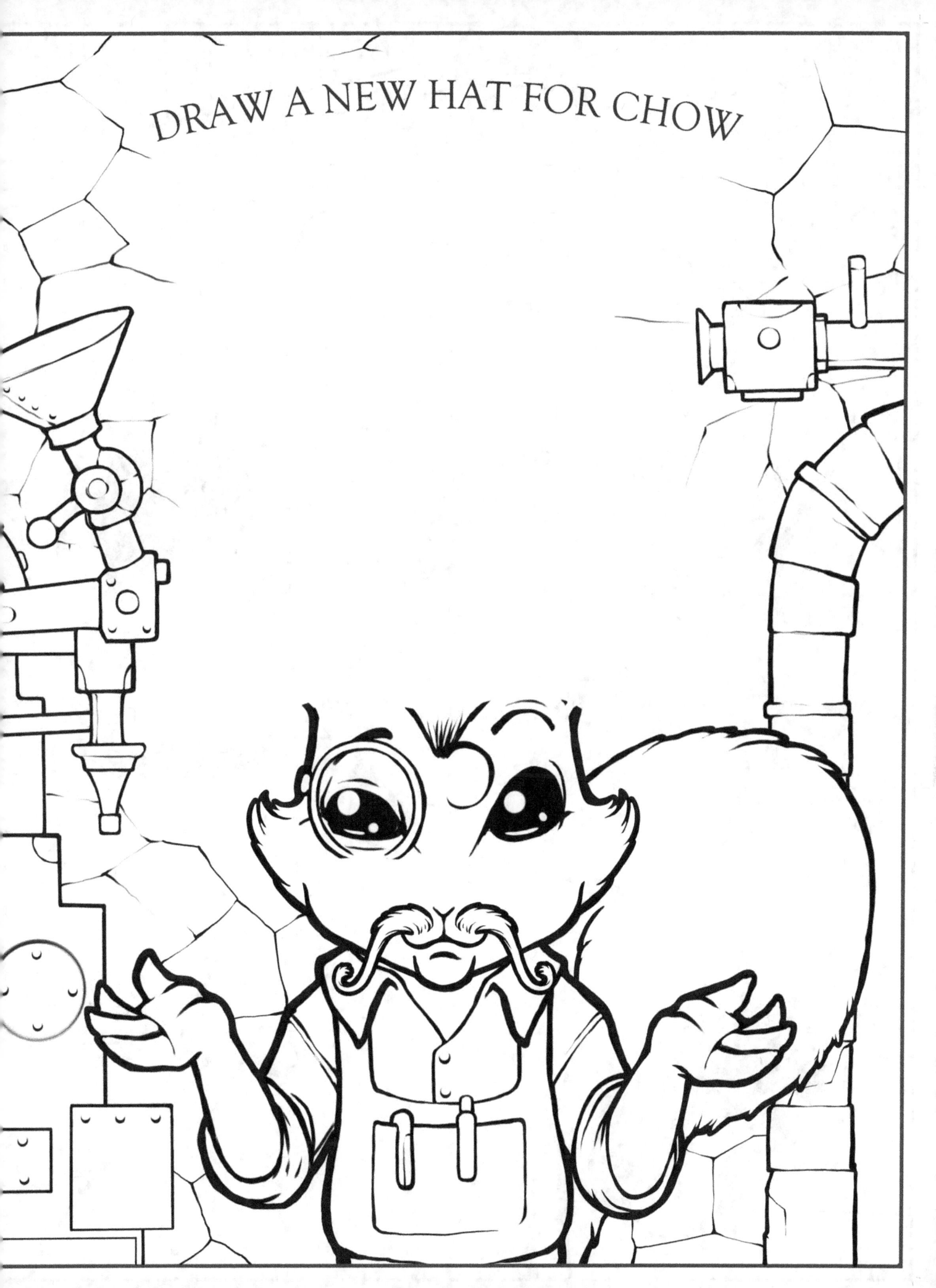

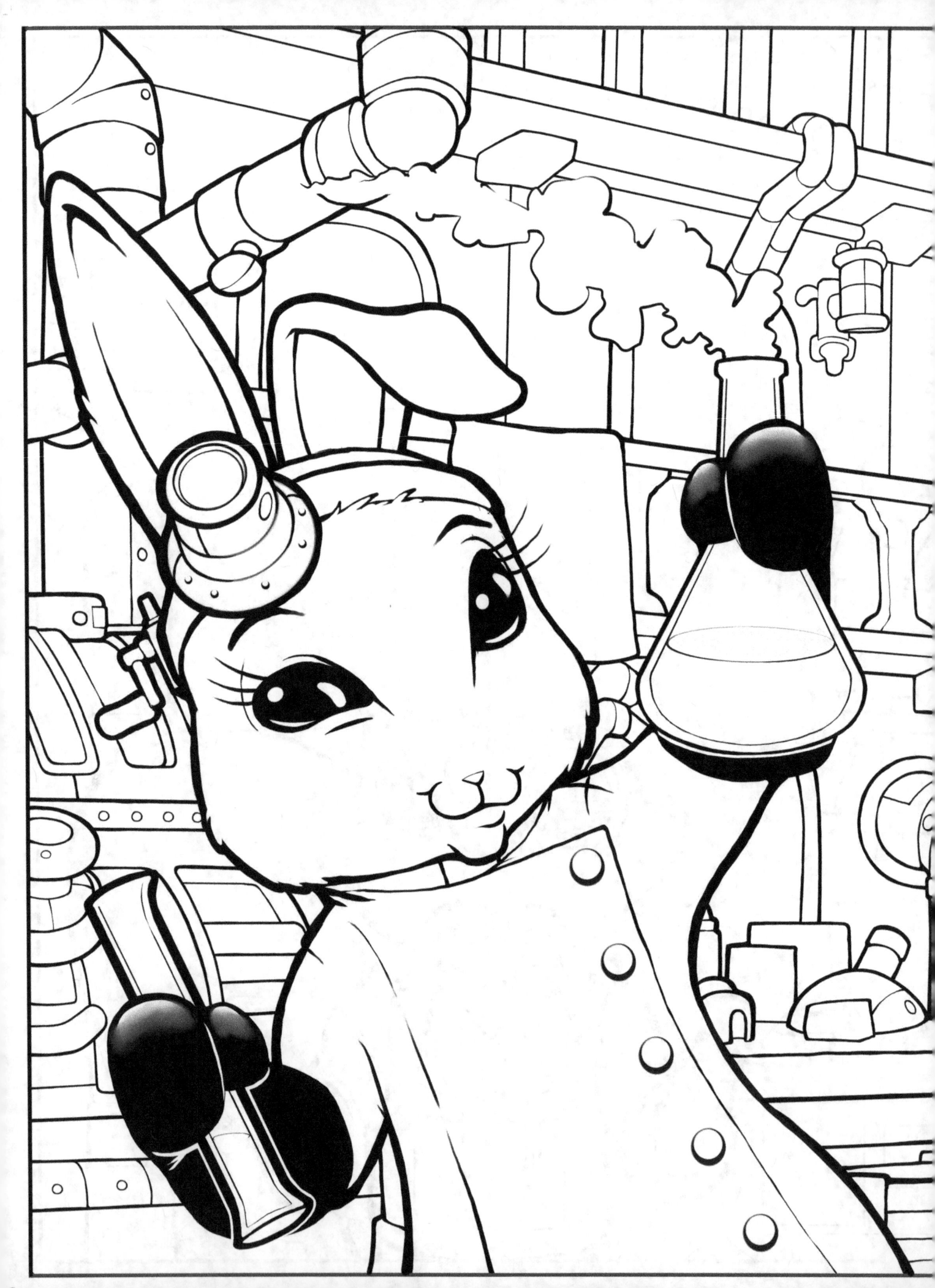

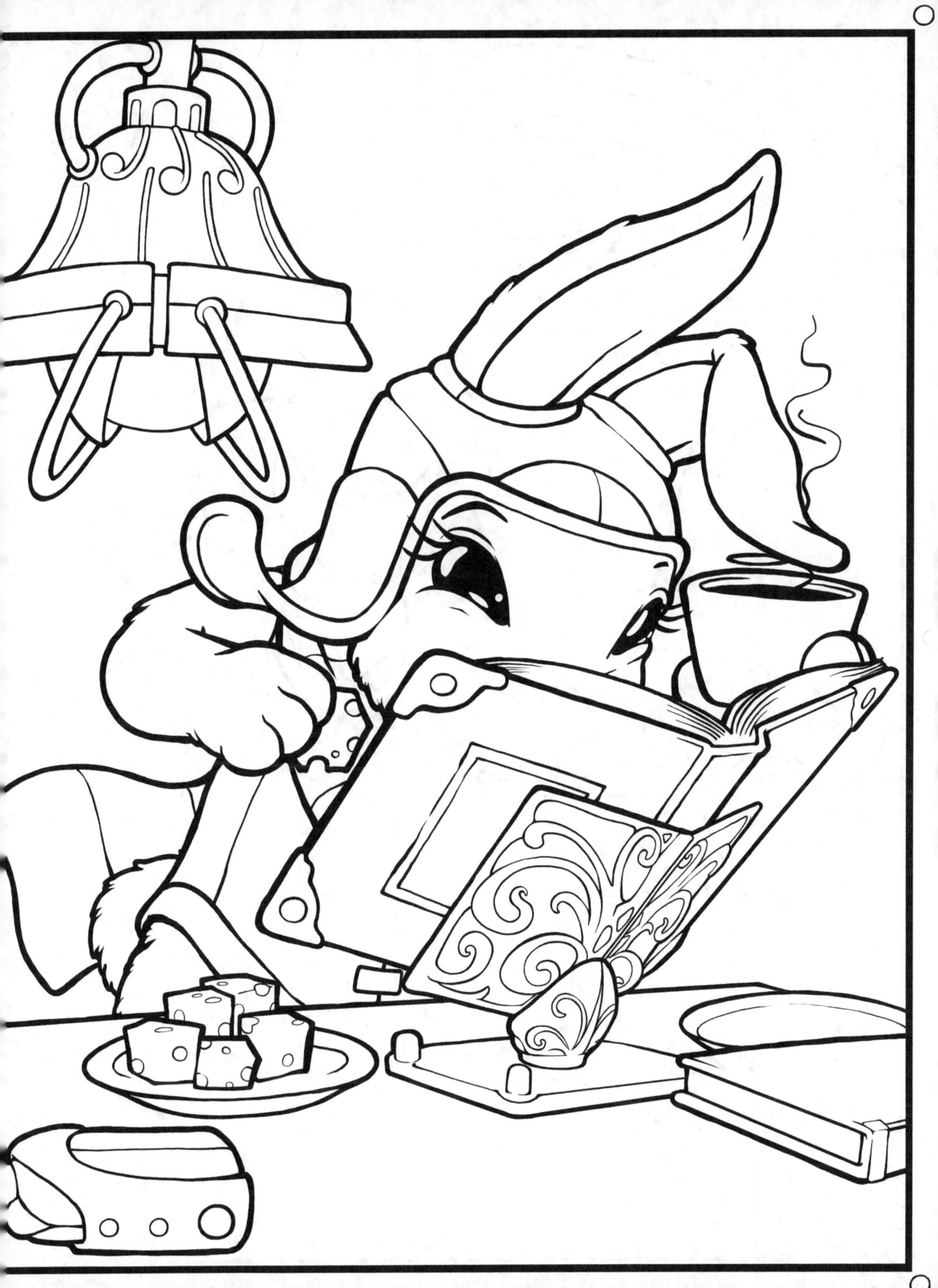

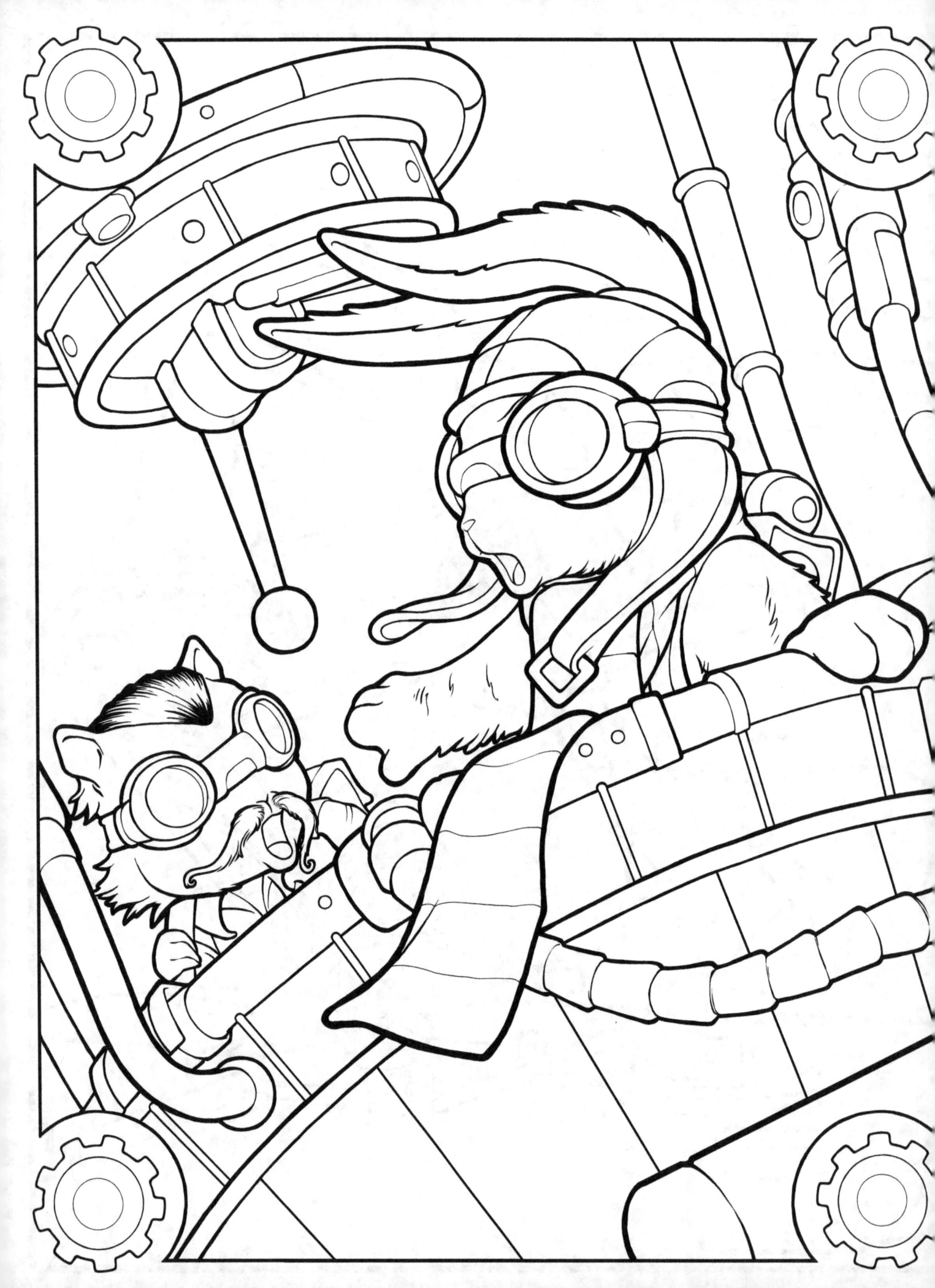

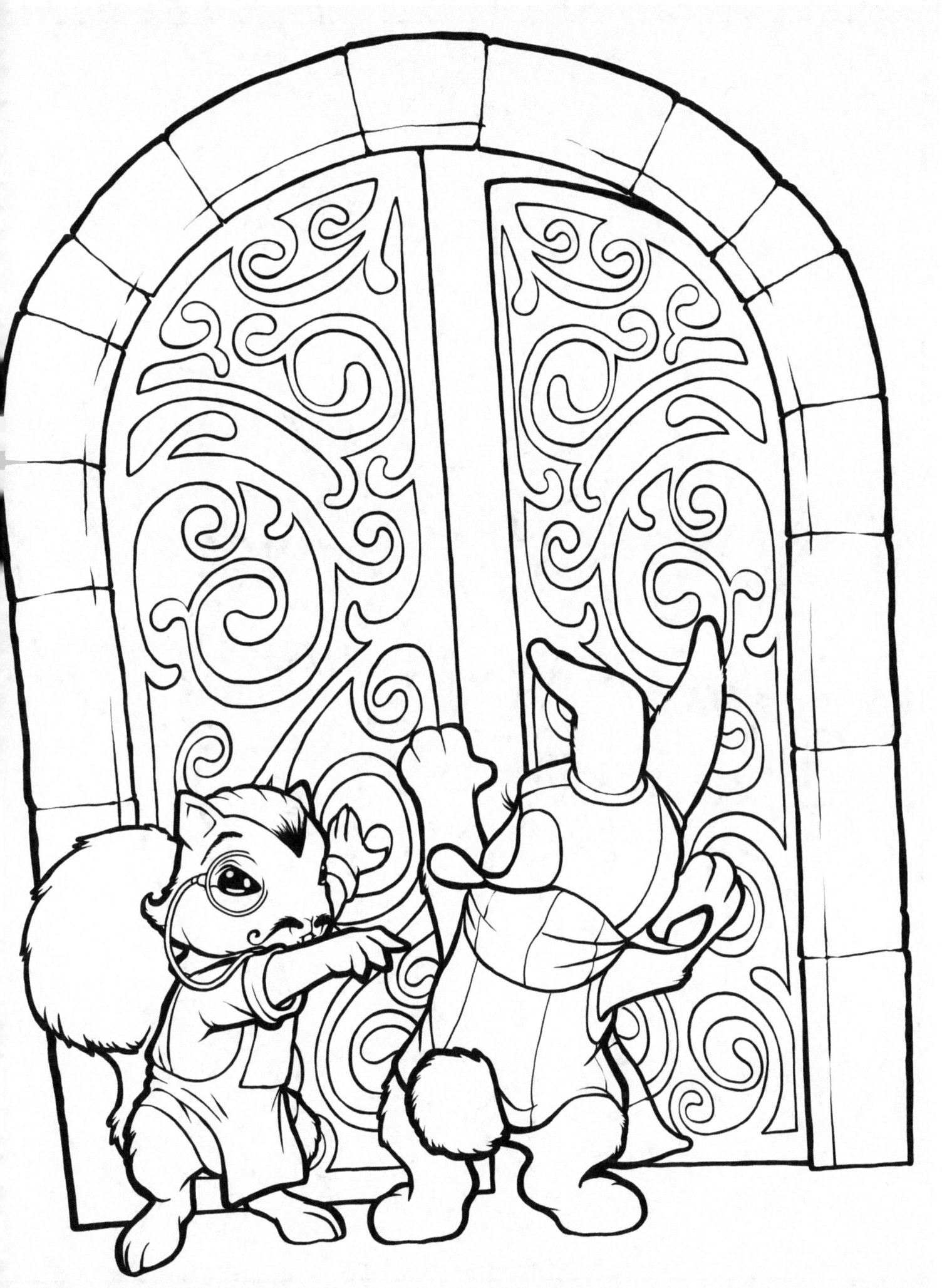

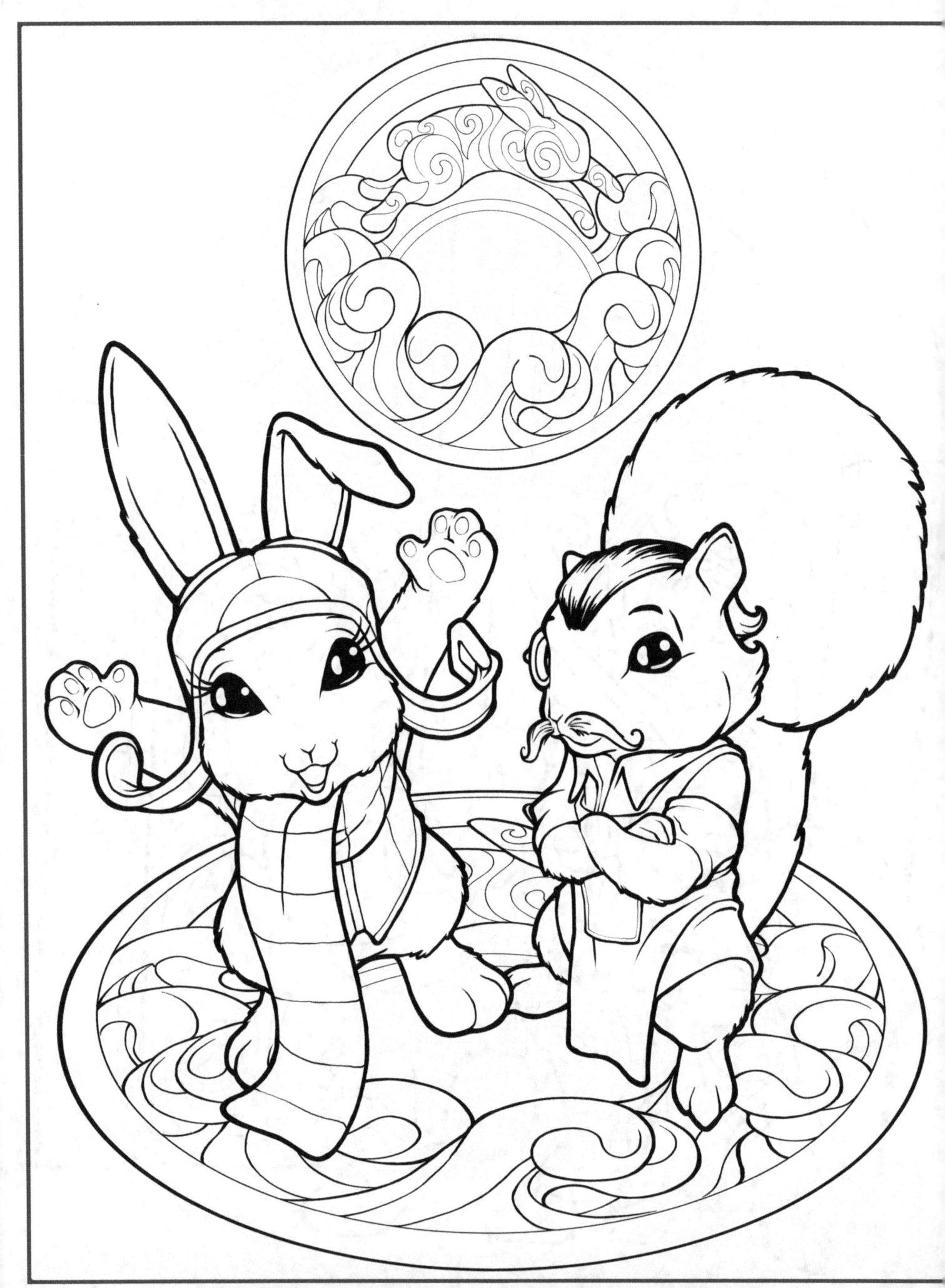

www.ingramcontent.com/pod-product-compliance
Lightning Source LLC
Chambersburg PA
CBHW060008230526
45472CB00008B/2002